I Can't Do This Anymore

Karen Hardy
with
Bryan Massey

Legacy Book Press LLC
Camanche, Iowa

This book is dedicated to all those who suffer and struggle with the disease of addiction and codependency.
May you find peace and healing.

Disclaimer:

This story is written from the perspective of Karen Hardy and Bryan Massey. The events are true, and some names have been changed due to privacy considerations.

Thank you to all those who have supported me through the writing of this book. Also, to those who listened to me endlessly struggle to figure out how to live knowing my son may die.

Stephen, I am beyond grateful for your endless presence and unwavering support. Words are not enough.

Table of Contents

I Am Your Disease
—Anonymous

I hate meetings. I hate Higher Powers. I hate anyone who has a program. To all who come in contact with me – I wish you death and I wish you suffering.

Allow me to introduce myself: I am the disease of ADDICTION – cunning, baffling, and powerful, that's me. I have killed millions and I am pleased. I love to catch you by surprise. I love pretending I am your friend and lover. I have given you comfort, have I not?

Wasn't I there when you were lonely? When you wanted to die? Didn't you call me? I was there. I love to make you cry. Better yet, I love when I make you so numb you can neither hurt nor cry. You cannot feel anything at all. This is true glory. I will give you instant gratification and all I ask of you is long-term suffering. I have always been there for you. When things were going right in your life, you invited me. You said you didn't deserve these good things, and I was the only one who would agree with you. Together we were able to destroy all things good in your life.

I am such a hated disease, and yet, I do not come uninvited. You choose to have me. So many have chosen me over power and peace.

More than you hate me, I hate all of you who have a 12-step program. Your programs, your meetings, your Higher Power – all weaken me, and I cannot function in the manner to which I am accustomed. Now, I must lie here quietly. You don't see me, but I am growing bigger than ever. I am here…and until we meet again, if we meet again, I wish you death and suffering.

Introduction

I started to write this book as a therapeutic tool, a way to "re-member" the insane details of the life we were leading. Friends and family didn't understand when one day I would tell them Bryan was doing well, in treatment, and the next time I spoke with them he had relapsed and was doing badly again. The response was so often, "What? But I thought he was doing so good?!" I would say, "Yeah, well, that was a week ago" ...and in my head, I would say, "You have no idea." How could they? So, I decided to chronicle the day to day-to-day life we all were living. I wanted both our experiences to be shared – side by side. I am not a writer as a profession, but I wanted this part of our story told. This book was initially self-published and a lot has evolved since that time.

You may have heard (or not) that addiction is a family disease. That means we all get sick. In our case, the family disease started with a generation before me and very possibly beyond. My father and Bryan's paternal grandfather both drank alcohol that greatly affected family members. So, my family of origin and Bryan's father's family of origin had a lot of dysfunction in it, and we brought that dysfunction into our children's lives. I won't go into too much of that history, but here is some context for Bryan's and my life leading up to the writing of this book.

On July 4, 2009, my youngest child, Bryan, then 18, was living with me. His father had moved to New York State from Massachu-setts where we lived. Bryan did not want to leave Massachusetts at that time, so he stayed with us. My husband, Stephen, and I were involved in volunteer work, and on this day, we were at a craft fair raising funds for our non-profit organization. Sometime in the afternoon, I received a call from Bryan telling me that he was in Boston and was going to spend the night there with friends to watch the fireworks. I was mad because he didn't ask, but rather he told me, and it felt risky and unsafe. He had not done anything like this before, and it bothered me. Bryan hadn't lived with me in many years; he had lived with his father. So, I was learning about what it had been like at his father's house.

In the middle of the night, I received a call that he was in the hospital because he had broken an ankle and would probably be there overnight. He was drunk, had gotten belligerent with an officer and almost got arrested. I went back to sleep. People said how strong I was to go back to sleep. I tried to believe it was strength, but never felt that was what it was. I was tired, and I remember thinking, *There's nothing I can do anyway, and I know he's safe.* At that time, I had no way of knowing how many nights I would go to sleep with that thought. I also had no way of knowing how many nights I would go to sleep with the thought, *Will I get a call from a hospital? Police? Morgue?* There came a time I did not even leave the ringer on at night. It feels a little selfish now, as I write this, that I was choosing my sleep over possibly knowing about the wellbeing of my son, but I had to be able to function at work.

When he came home from Boston, I told him he could not stay at our house if he was going to be engaging in this kind of behavior and disrespect.

Around this time, he had his wisdom teeth removed. I recall his reaction to the Percocet that he had been prescribed; he was goofy, silly, and kind of fun to be around. Looking back, though, I remember having pangs of irritation. The silliness didn't last for just a few minutes. The silliness endured for as long as the medication was present. I had the vague realization that his behavior was due to his reaction to the drugs, and I felt we might be encouraging him by laughing, and that wasn't good. I used the word vague because that is how I have experienced various levels of denial. It's like a small voice somewhere inside, or a fleeting thought or just a sense that something isn't quite right. Like when I had the niggle that he was smoking pot and I could kind of tell by his eyes, but then my brain said, "No, I don't think that's going on." Denial is a big word, and anyone who has been affected by this disease has probably experienced it, this includes the person using substances. I once heard the definition of denial perfectly stated as, "It's our way of protecting ourselves from a thought, experience, or information that we are not ready or able to face because it would be too overwhelming or painful." A defense. A protective factor for our senses, our heart. At the same time, denial protects us; it also enables other consequences and negative actions to occur.

For Christmas 2011, we all traveled to Mississippi for the holiday; we went on Christmas Day, and it was there that he said he experienced his first actual withdrawal. I remember him telling me that he thought he had the flu, that he felt sick. I bought him some over the counter medications to address those symptoms, but it wasn't until several years later that we both realized that that's what was happening.

Life went on. Bryan had moved to his dad's in New York in the spring of 2012. Bryan called me and said that he needed help, he was having a hard time with drugs, and was looking forward to going to Florida for treatment. When I asked why Florida, he said, "Because that's what came up when I started searching."

He went to treatment in Florida, did well, and I went down to have a family session. I remember telling my then-supervisor that he had gone off to treatment, and I was so happy and thought he would just get 'fixed up,' come back, and we would all move on. He scoffed a little, not in a mean way, but in a knowing way that I did not, that it would likely not be that simple. It was not the end, as we had hoped. Bryan has said that he had had similar thoughts about how the future would go after going to that treatment center, and he did not expect that it would be as hard to change as it has been.

His father moved to Florida, from New York, in 2014. It was a pretty spontaneous move for him; Bryan had lived with his father since about the age of 12. Bryan ended up moving to Florida with his father, and for the next three years, continued to struggle with his addiction as it progressed. In April 2016, he went to jail. There is a saying in 12 step programs about what would happen if one continues to use alcohol and drugs: "jails, institutions, or death." If you continue to use drugs, those are the options available. I felt like he had been in institutions, now going to jail, and there was only one option left. Life became increasingly difficult for us all. It was when he got out of jail that I decided to write this book. I had kept notes of all the various treatment programs he had been in and names of counselors, case managers, and house managers. It was overwhelming, and I don't know if I could even name all the places he has been to. He said he has been to 40+ treatment centers throughout south Florida and California. I went down several times over the three years he was there, and each time felt it could be the last time I saw him.

In April 2016, he went to jail. I felt like I had reached my limit of managing stress. I had been attending counseling regularly, was on Facebook support groups for moms and family members of those with addictions and tried to connect with some of them in person for added support. Stephen and I did our very best to carry on our lives with some normalcy, but in hindsight, it was still kind of foggy. I think my brain was always on Bryan, sometimes a little, sometimes a lot. He got out of jail July 30, and I decided to start keeping track of my thoughts and his and my daily functioning as best I could. I had the idea for this book to chronicle our lives for a year, not knowing what the year would bring, but I would do it no matter what.

It feels important to note that I studied psychology in school, worked at a prison and earned an addiction certification, and worked at a treatment program for addictions. Because of my background, it felt especially hard to accept that all of my education and experience did nothing to prevent or event detect this in my home and family. As I reflect, it seems obvious in hindsight, and I "should have known."

The format of this book is written to record what was happening for me on this side of our situation and what I know of that happened for him on his side. I told him I was writing this and asked if he would be interested in sharing his thoughts: he said yes. Neither of us knew how the upcoming year would go, and the input from his side was mostly based on communications I had with him and from him via Facebook, phone, or text. The left side of the page is my input; the right side is his. My hope is that people get a little sense of the insanity and struggle that occurs for all those involved with addiction. I do not believe that ours is the 'worst' of situations that are out there; the nightmare situations that families around the world suffer with addiction is beyond comprehension. The experiences we have been through were beyond our comprehension at the time. We continue to work toward recovery for our family; it is a daily effort. I pray this helps open some eyes and hearts to the great need for recovery efforts for individuals and their families.

Letters to Bryan

April 23, 2016

Dear Bryan,

I don't know if this is "the bottom," but the events of the last 24 hours seem to be an especially big deal and a possible bottom.

I am on vacation, with Stephen, the first real vacation we have taken in many years. Last night, our second night here, I fell asleep thinking about you falling asleep in a cell. I fell asleep thinking about the day you were running away from the police when they were doing a wellness check a couple weeks ago. The sound of your voice stuck in my head. There was a fear and desperation in your voice that hit me in a visceral way. It made me feel sick and so incredibly helpless. You are my son, and I've been raised to believe that my job is to protect and keep you safe...and I feel like I have not done my job. On those phone calls, I think you wanted me to do something for you though we both knew there wasn't anything I could possibly do.

Stephen and I walked from the hotel over to the local pizza shop for dinner, and when we came back, there was a police car in front of the hotel. There were only two other cars besides ours, and my brain was racing through why they might have been there...a notification maybe? Did something happen to you? I wondered how they would know where I was and why your dad didn't call me...how could something have happened in prison in one day? The police officer was at the desk, I don't really know why...but nothing was said to me! Then I felt crazy for thinking it had anything to do with you. According to your dad, you were calling him and Becky from the holding cell all night...did you really ask her not to go to detox?! Did you guys really get high at the hotel? Why would you ask her to not go to detox?! Sometimes I feel like you just tell me whatever you want, because you think it's what I want to hear. I'm tired...tired of trying to figure out "the truth" – it's like a moving target.

April 24, 2016

Dear Bryan,

I didn't tell you...we stopped at the Rite Aid the first night we got here because I forgot something. I was waiting in line looking around the store, and there was a Western Union Sticker in the window. I cringed and had a sad, sinking feeling. I now relate/ equate that to your desperate times. And I also learned yesterday that you stole from your dad's credit card. Stephen reminded me that you had tried to get me to order you a pizza using my card – were you going to steal from me too!? I am moving into an anger phase; maybe this is just somewhere to put the fear and energy that feels more productive in some weird way.

We are checking out of the hotel today – back to work tomorrow. Stephen just went to take a shower...I cried and realized I didn't want to cry in front of him today. I cannot stand to see the helpless, pained look on his face. He wants to help me, but he can't; I want to help you, but I can't. See how that goes? It trickles down and around and everyone is touched. I am soon going to let our family secret out...after all the sadness about Prince, I want to remind people that there are so many non-famous people struggling and dying every day!!! I think my life may be changing direction again soon. Another day, thinking about how you are – your dad said you guys used after you got out of detox – so you may be a little sick in jail right now. Oh well...consequences.

I pray and pray for you to be able to have some clarity in your head, that we can all live a wonderful life. I love you so and want all good things for you.

April 25, 2016

Dear Bryan,

Well, we have entered the "jail thing." It seems surreal…I was so happy to hear your voice, so happy…and then I felt like some of the old chaos started…especially the part of you asking me to get a message to someone else's mom. I totally feel for all of us moms – as well as all of our children – but there is a whole lot of self-centeredness and manipulation that comes with addiction and maturing…I did look for that mom and couldn't find her. I'm kinda pissed, actually, that I spent money on a phone call with you, for you to try to help someone else in prison! I am all for helping others – but I can tell you from firsthand experience that unless I help me first, I cannot adequately help anyone.

I am going to court this morning with one of my clients and his family. It is a very sad situation and non-addiction related, but I feel some irony about this.

I will try to write more later; somehow, I feel like this is helping me a little bit right now. Thank God because I need all the help I can get!

April 27, 2016

Dear Bryan,

Today you go to court – closed circuit from jail. I have had to work really hard to maintain my focus on work. I almost started crying yesterday during a session; I am training with a supervisor, and I felt like he kept telling me I wasn't doing it right…he kept correcting me. I so want to not get sucked into the abyss of sadness that threatens to overwhelm me, always. I continue to push forward and try to maintain my balance in all the areas of my life. I did hear from Becky today – she said your dad is taking her to rehab today – I continue to pray and ask others to pray for you both…and we are, and they are. I have to work today but I am anxious to hear the outcome of your hearing. I did not set up an account, so hope it's not that hard…I may just ask your dad to keep me posted. I love you so much…I am so worried that you will have a difficult time staying focused on your own recovery if you don't stay in jail – I know you are so worried about Becky, but by staying focused on her, you take the focus off yourself.

Prayers continue…

May 24, 2016

Dear Bryan,

I feel like I am getting my life back – I am working hard in therapy, continuing to attend Naranon, am active on a site for moms of addicts, and plan to attend SMART recovery meetings. I have run two 5K's since breaking my ankle in March, and today I rode a 47 minute ten-mile bike ride that felt great! I write you as often as I can and look forward to talking to you Friday…I pray all the time that you can find the strength to face your fears and pain and get to the point where you realize there is so much more this life and work has to offer. I want to be the best role model for you that I can be…I even have hopes and plans to do some fundraising for addiction in a bike ride way!

I love you so much and will continue to fight this fight!

Who's Who

Stephen – Bryan's Stepdad, my husband

Heather – Bryan's sister, my daughter

Jeff – Heather's husband

Alec – Stephen's son

Beth – Stephen's daughter

Bill – Bryan's father

Becky – Bryan's ex-girlfriend

Catherine – An advocate in Florida who helps families who are dealing with addiction

Sarah – Bryan's half-sister, Bill's daughter

Hannah – Bryan's niece, Sarah's daughter

Sharon – the woman who called 911 the day he overdosed and nearly died

Doug – good friend of Bryan's from rehab

Eric – a kid from high school who Bryan played sports with

Brendan – Bryan's roommate in New York

Sam – Owner of a treatment center

Lenny – Clinical Director at a treatment facility in Florida.

July 2016

Saturday July 30, 2016 – a.m.

A.M. Text:

I'm outtttttttt!!! I'm going to call shortly."

Yay!!!! He is out of jail…it has been a long few months, but the anticipation and anxiety do not end. He is now out, and the fear is creeping back…what if, what if…

How will he do?

What will happen now?

I am a bit hopeful; he has sounded good these past months, clear and focused and saying all "the right things."

Is it talk? Is it true?

Will he be able to do what he says?

Evening:

I hope you are enjoying the day.

He sounded good every time that I talked to him through the day; making plans for his next steps, sounds committed.

I hope……

Sunday July 31, 2016

He got high sometime – got his car, went out with his girlfriend, used heroin.

"I think I need to go somewhere for like two weeks."

What??!! It has been a matter of hours!!

I told him that there are two people who I know in Florida who know about resources there; someone would be in touch with him.

> "Awesome. I love you so much mother.
> I really think I might do inpatient."

I couldn't believe how quickly he got high; for three months he sounded good, healthy, and adamant that he was going to change and have a different life when he left jail.

Within hours, hopes were dashed.

"Keep me posted"

> "I will, I am at the doctor's now. I'm in a bad mood.
> I'll call you after and let you know what's going on."

I felt like his willingness to go to treatment, and considering inpatient, was a positive step. Hope returned a bit.

"I love you."

4:00 p.m. text – "Any update from the doctor?"

> NO ANSWER

9:53 p.m. text – "Going to sleep, rest well."

> NO ANSWER

What is going on?!

> …nothing

August 2016

Monday August 1, 2016

1:22 p.m. text – "I am with you…I love you more than I can say"

"I love you too – I'm with Catherine now looking at places…it's hard, I don't want to be locked in again."

"Try to stay open minded"

"Yeah, I know. I love you Mom, I'm going somewhere."

No return calls after attempts. I texted, "confused, you won't talk to me?!"

"I will, I fell asleep. I'm sorry. I'll call you around 5. I feel so embarrassed and depressed."

Those words hurt…I feel his pain.

"I understand…you can still make good choices today – regardless of yesterday"

I sent repeated texts to find out more…no answers. I went to Nara-non. He said he was at a facility but wouldn't say where. No calls.

"Ok, I'll call soon – I think I'm going to the treatment center Catherine mentioned." (A supposedly reputable facility)

I found out later that he ended up going to an IOP, Intensive Outpatient Program, that was not reputable according to people I have met in Florida.

Tuesday August 2, 2016

7:10 p.m.

He sent a picture of himself with a cat. This is the first photo I have seen of him since February, except his jail arrest photo.

8:55 p.m.

"Any updates?"

Nothing all day until 9:11 p.m.

"No, I'm going to sleep. I'm going in tomorrow for sure cuz I don't like this area."

"Let me know in the a.m. I love you – I know you can make the best decision for yourself."

Trying to pass on reassurance that I don't fully believe.

"I will. I love you so much Mom I am fine again. I miss you and I'll see you soon."

Wednesday August 3, 2016

11:01 a.m. text:

"You awake yet?"

"yeah, working on something"

"I have a 12:00 appointment and done at 1:00."

"Ok, we shall catch up then."

(For me, shall is a trigger word…It seems that is a word he uses more when he is using.).

Sometime later:

"any updates?

"Talking to a guy from that treatment facility"

By 6:00 p.m., there was no progress; he had not gone anywhere, changing his mind. I felt like I was holding my breath all day waiting to see what he did. I ended up talking to him on the phone and confronted him about this, and he hung up the phone on me.

"You hung up on me?! The ice is so thin you might want to think very carefully about these choices."

6:19 p.m.

"I don't want to argue, that's not helping anything…I'm not using or plotting to use. I'm safe. I'm sorry this is just pushing me further."

"Ok – I will not call you. Do not call me…it's pushing me too. Let me know when it is figured out, and I can forget about planning your funeral."

So much fear – so much unknown – how do I stay positive? Hopeful?

"You don't have to plan a funeral."

8:24 p.m.

"Good night, I love you." Even though I get so angry, scared really, I can't not tell him I love him...what if he died?!

8:45 p.m.

"I love you too – good night."

Thursday August 4, 2016

6:22 a.m.

"Good morning. I love you. Sorry I haven't really trusted you….I will try harder. . Scared to death is all…drugs make it hard for your brain to be clear."

"I know, it's okay, I love you mom. I'm sorry too. . I'm not trying to make things harder. ... I just know where my head is at and my heart."

7:11 a.m.

"Hope you had a good day. I love you so much. Tomorrow the Olympics start, fyi. I had a counselor session today where we talked about keeping the situation lighter, with love. I decided I wanted to try to talk about other things besides addiction and treatment."

16

"Yeah, I did. I'm leaving Becky I guess."

"I know how hard this is and has been, even if you think I don't care about your feelings about Becky, I do. Take care of yourself."

"I'm trying."

Friday August 5, 2016

7:42 a.m.

"good morning...I love you."

6:50 p.m.

"I hope you had a good day. Wishing you all good things. I love you."

NOTHING ALL DAY UNTIL...

8:03 p.m.

"Thank you, mother, I love you very much."

(Apparently his phone was broken, he called from his dad's house phone.)

I noticed that he sounded more relaxed in the evening – had a relaxing day. That led me to think that he had been using something; one does not go from incredibly stressed, anxious, and confused to relaxed, chatty, and calm in two days with limited coping skills...ugggh...

Saturday August 6, 2016

Stephen and I spent some time with Heather and Jeff; did not hear from Bryan.

Sunday August 7, 2016

10:33 a.m.

"Good morning. I love you."

"I love you tons."

1:33 p.m.

"What's going on?"

"Not much. Cleaning, doing laundry and what not. So, a relaxing day today."

"Did you get your phone fixed? I am flying to NJ soon…"

"Yeah, I did thank God. I went to a meeting last night, which was nice."

I was going to attend a three-day training for work.

Monday August 8, 2016

"Great! Good morning…love you."

"Morning, I'm about to go to IOP – I love you."

IOP was ok, he said, will be meeting with a counselor. He says his triggers for using are not avoidance of past events. He said he used last week because he thought it would be fun. But he couldn't tolerate how upset everyone got and what it does to others.

I am at EMDR training in NJ for 3.5 days. He has been staying at his dad's; the arguing and paranoia has begun, and he said he will start looking to move out, where? Who knows? Uggghh!!

9:50 p.m.

"I love you mother so freaking much it kills me not seeing you like ever."

I was already asleep…

Thursday August 9, 2016

5:45 a.m.

"I know I miss you so much, it has been too long…

5:10 p.m.

I called.

"Hey I'm playing video games at my friend's. He's dropping me off soon, I'll call you around 6, sound well?"

"Sound well." Those are more trigger words...an alarm in me. His language and chosen phrases are different when he is using. He may not be 'high- high' – but the thought is, if he starts using anything, what's next?!

Always the thought somewhere inside, *"Will I get a call? Will he get bad H?"*

Later in the day, he was arguing with his girlfriend and his father and said, "I'm really struggling. I'm ok Mom, it's just hard."

Always...fear...I want to make that stop.

Wednesday August 10, 2016

I was traveling all day, back from NJ training. I finally talked to him while I was on the plane – the captain was talking, and I had a hard time hearing. Bryan was talking about his future plans – IOP owner had said he would make him house manager if he did well....in a few months. WTF!!!! After 2-3 months? That doesn't sound right!!

He went and did equine therapy. "I was scared the last time I was supposed to do this – I'm going to do it though."

Thursday August 11, 2016

Nothing bad or noteworthy during the day. At night, I looked out the window and thought I saw a car in the driveway. My brain jumped to, "Is that a police car? Maybe they are here to tell me in person...."

Text: "good night, I love you."

"I love you too."

I guess he's ok...I feel like there is something really wrong with me for thinking like that.

Friday August 12, 2016

The Clinical Director called; we talked about Bryan and his treatment. I shared some history and thoughts about treatment concerns about a halfway house that they will soon open.

I talked to Bryan; he sounded good. He did not sound manic and not like he was bullshitting me; he sounded goal oriented.

"Getting tired of Dad; he always follows my moves on the phone. I am going to get a job, get my own phone and work toward being on my own. I know it will take time."

Happy mom going to sleep…these nights are few and far between.

Saturday August 13, 2016

I went to a craft event for Stephen's Reiki business. We were there all day, and Bryan and I played phone tag. We finally connected about 6:00 p.m. He said he might be getting a job at Subway.

Sunday August 14, 2016

I sent a string of emoji's. We face-timed on the phone – I haven't seen him since February. He has gained weight and resembles my brother quite a bit. He saw an ad for a place we had visited when he was younger, and we talked briefly about our memories of that time. It was nice to have some conversation that felt 'normal.'

11:02 a.m.

"I have an interview Tuesday at Subway!!!!"

He talked about going to court the next day – supposed to testify against a kid who stole from his dad. He felt like a hypocrite doing this and knows what jail is like. He hates the idea of doing that to someone.

Monday August 15, 2016

I worked, made phone calls. Put out information to organizations that we want to raise money for them by doing a bike ride next year. Stephen and I are planning to raise money for overdose awareness by riding our bikes.

8:11 a.m. – Going to court, still feeling bad. Didn't sleep much.

10:53 a.m.

"Court is done – no need to testify. The kid will
probably cut a deal; I'm relieved. I'm bringing
Becky to a job interview."

8:39 p.m. – Text:

"Good night, I love you. Rest Well."

"I love you too mother, sleep good.
I want to live Mom – I have a purpose…a job."

Tuesday August 16, 2016

I'm trying to set up a call with Bryan and the Clinical Director for Wednesday.

He called in the evening, wanting to vent – I focused on just listening. He said he knows what he needs to do – frustrated living with his dad.

"Dad said, 'You have to be a man
and you can't be so emotional.'"

Bryan said, "That his is just stupid. I think
that's the worst advice anyone has ever given me."

Wednesday August 17, 2016

I talked to the Clinical Director – he sounds like he is working with Bryan on helping with his treatment and "allowing him to also work a job so he can get out of his dad's house."

Today I feel some peace – knowing that he is trying and wants to live. I know Noah wanted to live too…at least I feel like he hasn't just given up.

"Mom, I didn't sleep all night – there is too
much chaos around…Becky and Dad"

8:35 p.m. – text:

"Mom, Becky od'd Mom. She was out for
30 minutes. Please Mom I'm done I
give up on this stuff Mom...."

8:39 p.m. – text:

"Is she with you?! Where are you?!"

Nothing as of 9:05 p.m....I can't breathe...

10:30 p.m.

"I'm going to jail mom – on possession charges.
I will beat them cause of the good Samaritan
law. If bonded out, I'll go to the good treatment center."

"Ok. I love you, stay strong. When do you know about bond?"

"I love you please help get me out Mom.
I'll know tonight or tomorrow morning. I'll even
make payments if I can make it to work tomorrow."

"Treatment not work...I know you want to work but, I do have to
work tomorrow and decide about the trip I booked...where will
you be? I will help if I can. Maybe you should come to Maine."

"ok, I will. I love you get me out I will come there."

Things change fast...

Thursday August 18, 2016

11:16 a.m. –

I know you love Becky, but that relationship is killing you and
her!!! Call me when you can. I have a 12:00 appointment...talk
soon...Love you so much.

He called from jail last night at 11:30 p.m. – I had no money on
the phone, so no way to answer – uggghhh! I texted his dad to see
if he knew anything. Finally, at 12:30 I took melatonin to sleep.

Friday August 19, 2016

I woke up at 5:30 a.m. I talked to the treatment center, Catherine talked to me, Bill, and treatment center. I had a doctor appointment and saw two clients today.

I was exhausted but pulled it off!

Bryan got out today, no bond, goes to court 9-16-16.

I canceled my vacation plans – so sad. I offered for him to come up here after his court date.

He was in shock after getting home – Becky had overdosed quickly; he said he was going to use but saw what happened to her and called 911. He is sad and devastated and confused and scared.

He may come to Maine. He is talking to the Clinical Director at IOP tomorrow.

8:06 a.m. – text:

"You awake? Love you, hope you rested. My first appointment isn't until 10:15 today."

9:12 a.m. – text:

"What's your address? What's the zip?"

"Call if you want"

I gave him the address…

"I'm heading to my appointment soon – IOP. Ok I will."

I had appointments all afternoon – and called him on my way home at 6:45 p.m. He and Becky were at Bill's – he was hemming and hawing and saying he was deciding what to do…He had been at work – she overdosed again, ended up in the hospital, they called him and he left his job.

Sometime overnight they went to a detox.

8:58 p.m.

"Goodnight, I hope you can rest. I love you."

"I love you so much Mom."

I'm so scared...I love him...it doesn't change anything.

"I made it I love you. I'm safe."

"Made it where?! I am so glad you are safe – I love you so much."

Saturday August 20, 2016

5:57 a.m.

A marketer from a program in West Palm Beach got them drugs – they went to detox apparently.

It makes by brain spin...how can this be??!!

I went and had breakfast with Jeff at the restaurant that Heather works at – got home at 11:30 a.m. I spent most of the day on the phone talking to people about how to help Bryan and to get away from Becky. Nice, helpful people who work hard to help all the kids who are in Florida trying to get treatment.

I got a call from someone saying that Bryan was at a program. I didn't know if it was a real person from a real program...I was very skeptical.

I was exhausted...sad...scared...

Overwhelmed...confused.

Sunday August 21, 2016

I went for a run/walk with Stephen, wrote notes for work, had coffee with a new friend whose daughter is addicted to heroin. I had lunch with another friend and while there, talked to Bryan – he had called and left a message while I was at the first friend's place.

"Hi Mom. I am using my safe call and just want you to know I'm ok. I am staying here no matter what and I just want to get better. I really feel like there's a reason I'm still here – I

should or could be dead by now. To be honest –
when Becky overdosed, I was going to use,
but couldn't find a vein – if I had used, I think
we both would be dead. Becky was moved to a
higher level of care, and I told her if
she leaves I will not follow her."

After that call, I was able to more fully relax – went home and crashed – so tired and relieved. I went for a real nice swim in the late afternoon and have plans to go on a nice boat ride with Stephen, Alec, Heather, and Jeff tomorrow in Bar Harbor. I plan to fully enjoy it and have some hope back.

Thank you guides and Angels.

Monday August 22, 2016

We went to Bar Harbor today. Heather asked that we not talk about Bryan at all – I slipped a little, but it didn't seem to be a problem.

I didn't hear from him – he was going to call after signing a release.

Did he leave?

Forget?

Change his mind?

Not want to talk to me?

Why wouldn't he call?

NOTHING

Tuesday August 23, 2016

I went for a bike ride with Stephen this morning – got some work done on the website for my private practice and had three appointments.

By 7:49 p.m. I got a call…

"Hi Mom – I'm doing good. I'm going to stay.
When I see my counselor, we will sign a

release of information. I don't think I can talk
to Dad for a while – he is so rude and disrespectful.
I am going to stay – I think Becky might not.
I want to sign up for school – I want to
have a goal. I got a sponsor, too."

"Maybe just take it one day at a time and get some clean time first – goals are good."

(I'm really just scared it's too much for him)

But he's safe so I can relax a bit.

Wednesday August 24, 2016

It was mostly a good day for me – I walked the dogs, baked banana bread, and saw a few clients.

I thought Bryan was going to call with his counselor. By 8:45 I hadn't heard and called Bill. Bryan had called him…he met with his dad and the counselor apparently…I found out after the fact.

NOTHING

Feeling confused and disappointed.

Thursday August 25, 2016

I worked on my website, wrote some assessments for work – made chocolate chip cookies. I talked to my mom. Called the facility about 11:30 and asked to talk to Bryan or his counselor.

They could not 'confirm or deny' that he was there, but she would have someone call if they could.

Bill said that he stopped in to bring cereal and ended up having a session with him and the counselor.

Friday August 26, 2016

I worked for most of the day – I called the treatment center where Bryan was, left two messages, and received one call back that "'a message would be passed along." I didn't hear anything back. It just didn't seem right…

Finally, Bryan called at 9:00 p.m.…Becky was somewhere with him, in a common area. I told him I was confused; thought he was going to call this week with the counselor.

> He said, "I like it here and will call for sure on Monday. I'm not supposed to use the phone without the counselor. I can't call till Monday. No, I didn't get any of the messages that you called."

I do not have a good feeling about this…. should I leave things alone? Are they just really busy there? Should I expect a call back? He said that he will call, will that happen?

Why are he and Becky at the same place? It sounded like they were arguing...

Will he stay or leave?

Will she?

Saturday August 27, 2016

Beth went into labor during the night and went to the hospital about 5:30 a.m. We left to go see her and got to the hospital at 9:30 – she had the baby about 10:30 a.m.

> 12:28 p.m.

> Bryan called, "Hi Mom, can you order me a pizza? Someone stole my food."

I told him that Beth had her baby – he sounded surprised and almost as if he had forgotten that was happening. It may have made him realize that life was going on and people are growing and changing.

> "Oooooh wow!! That's amazing – tell her I will call when I can – if I can get approved."

Sunday August 28, 2016

I went on a 20-mile bike ride with Stephen. 12:03 p.m. – missed call. I was working in the office and forgot my phone.

I decided to book another trip to Florida. I just want to see him....I miss him...it is so hard.

4:50 p.m.

"Hi Mom, I should be meeting with my counselor tomorrow."

Monday August 29, 2016

I worked at home....Naranon meeting after grocery shopping.

One of the only regular meeting members who attended that meeting had her last day. Jeff came and he was a guest speaker.

7:03 p.m.

"I didn't see my counselor today – I guess I have to sign up and I didn't know. You are going to be here at the same time Sarah and Hannah will be here. I am hoping I get to see them."

Heather and Jeff came to the house for dinner. I heard from Heather that Sarah does not want to see Bryan or for Hannah, her daughter, to see him...how ignorant!

Tuesday August 30, 2016

Had a 9:30 client and it was a mom of a child with an addiction. As we were ending the phone rang, from Florida...

10:59 a.m.

"Hi Mom – I'm having a hard time. Becky took 2 pregnancy tests – 1 positive, 1 negative. I don't know the truth!"

"If Becky leaves, I will cry and pray, I will call you later Mom."

He plans to stay where he is no matter what. Eventually thinking of coming to New England, Boston, maybe a halfway house. He wants to live. He wants to stay in Florida until his court case is done.

"Ok, if you can't call, I will cry and pray too."

"No Mom, please don't cry!"

7:43 p.m.

"I don't know what is really going on – I have no idea who my counselor is now – mine left, but I will be ok no matter what. I don't want to lose my family – I can't keep doing this – you're coming down in a couple weeks and I can't be worrying about Becky and you – I want to have my family."

I hear a difference in his tone – I hear a commitment and determination that I haven't heard in a long time. I want him to live. I feel hopeful with some lingering fear and concern.

Wednesday August 31, 2016

I called twice again today to try to connect with a staff person – left a message with a counselor. Later, I left a message with the receptionist who was bringing my message to the Clinical Director. As of 3:30 p.m., no return call – this is at least the fourth call I've made and no return call.

10:45 p.m.

Bill called – he was supposed to meet with Bryan and the counselor, but they went for an outing.

Did Bryan not sign a release? Does he not want to talk to anyone? Bill has talked to them…. feeling confused and left out.

September 2016

Thursday September 1, 2016

I worked during the day. I was irritated that the facility didn't call back yet. What kind of a place is this? That is not professional!

Is he really there?

How can they sound nice and as if they plan to return calls and assure me they will, then nothing!?

I talked to Bryan briefly, but no details of what is going on. I did not feel comfortable and am left to just keep waiting.

Friday September 2, 2016

8:32 a.m.

"Mom, I think I have to get out of here. I haven't seen a counselor in 2 weeks.

"Do you want me to make a call and set something up? If I do, will you leave?"

"Yes – I will go – I won't be able to call again. And can you set something up for Becky?"

The urgency of this situation left me feeling like I was in a race for his life.

I called Catherine and Lenny (he is from a recommended treatment facility). Then I called his dad. I had five client appointments throughout the day. It was decided that Bill would go pick him up and bring him to Lenny's facility.

4:14 p.m. – phone call

Bryan, what happened?! Why didn't you go?!

"I decided I don't need to go to treatment.
I'm gonna do the program of AA."

What's that? (thinking it was some different treatment program)

"Alcoholics Anonymous. I got a sponsor last
night and you don't even care!

"What happened to you saying your family is the most important
thing and you want to get better?!"

"What happened to you saying you weren't gonna try to control
me anymore?!"

He hung up…

By the time Bill had gotten there, they had deemed one of the
houses, a halfway house (as opposed to a treatment center?), and
Bryan and Becky decided to stay. They were staying there with
two other couples and a tech or two in the house. Often, techs are
people with less than six months of clean or recovery time; not
the most stable of situations.

I was pissed, confused, disappointed. What did I miss?! Is he using
again? Why is he doing this? Was I in denial all week thinking
he changed?

Saturday September 3, 2016

I went for a 5K run with Stephen and Jeff. Jeff decided to run
with us at the last minute; he won second place in his age group!
It was fun. I came in last with Stephen. It was ok; I felt good that
I got out and moved and wasn't sitting around moping.

NOTHING

We watched the movie *"Concussion"* and dozed in the afternoon.
Stephen and Jeff went for a swim; too cold for me!

We had some good food from a Greek truck in town.

I texted Bill to see if he knew anything. "They decided to leave that place and decided it was dangerous."

I was so sad and still confused about Bryan. I talked to a friend of mine, and we commiserated about our kids. I am glad I have a friend here who understands as a mom.

Sunday September 4, 2016

Went for a 20-mile bike ride with Stephen.

I told him I felt like deja vu, from when we were in Massachusetts, riding our bikes on Rt. 5 where we used to live. We had been talking about Bryan and the same kind of issues, six years ago? What should I do? I don't even know what to say at this point. Stephen said, "Just text him and check in, let him know you love him." I did that. "Just checking in – I love you – I don't understand all this and don't know if I ever will."

> He called, "Hi Mom." The call was a bit tentative, no apologies on either side. It was almost as if we knew there were not any apologies necessary or helpful at this point. It seemed an unspoken understanding that we both are struggling.

Stephen and I went to the movies, did some shopping for Jeff's 30th birthday coming up. Heather asked if we wanted to go out with her. We met in Farmington and had a beer and some snacks. It was a nice two-hour visit.

I talked to Bryan a couple more times; he had been working on another treatment program.

> "I found a place – going tomorrow. I really hate it here in Florida; there is so much greed and they don't really care about us. I know what I need to do, and I want to get better. I don't want to become institutionalized.

"You don't have to, but use the institutions to get help, then you can live your life."

Monday September 5, 2016 – Labor Day

20-mile bike ride again this morning. Worked on taxes, ate lunch. We rested and watched TV then went to Sam's Club – talked and texted with Bryan.

10:42 a.m. – he called

"I'm getting picked up to go to the program." We talked about 15 minutes. "I'm going to work with a sponsor. I'm gonna stay at least 30 days, maybe more… I don't want to use anymore – it's not fun."

3:53 p.m.

"I'm here Mom. The owner picked me up – I am going to sign a release and we will have sessions. Maybe you can even come and speak on Monday when you're here…"

Feeling cautiously optimistic about yet another program. Is it reputable? How long will he stay? 'People' (family) are coming around – but I haven't talked to them in months – fair weather friends…feeling resentful.

Tuesday September 6, 2016

Walked the dogs in the a.m.

I worked on my website. I called a Task Force in Florida to report abuse about one of the treatment centers where Bryan had been.

I had three client appointments.

12:50 p.m.

"Any updates on the ROI?"

"On what?

"Release of Information."

"Got it, we're good."

"Ok, good – I have a 1:30, 3, and 4 today."

"Wow, busy day."

Went to dinner with Heather and Jeff for his 30th birthday.

No other calls or contact for the remainder of the day.

Wondering if this program will be any better.

Wednesday September 7, 2016

8:02 a.m.

"Hey good morning! I thought you only had your phone on weekends. How are you feeling this morning?"

8:51 a.m.

"Not great honestly, but ok and me too, I guess I was wrong though…was misinformed."

He had started to talk about going somewhere else. I called insurance and got a list of in-network places.

"They told us to leave, that they felt that they couldn't help us." (He and Becky were at the same place.)

"Where are you going? Why not in-network?"

"Thankfully I set something up, out of being scared of that."

"I found a place…I had no time to make a decision."

I asked a few questions…no answers until:

6:20 p.m.

"I'm at the Center. I'll make my safe call to you. I love you a ton. Thank God, we made it somewhere."

Stephen and I went to see a showing of *Generation Found,* a documentary about recovery high schools. It made me feel happy and sad at the same time. Wishing Bryan had had an opportunity for

34

something like this.

How long will he stay this time?

Thursday September 8, 2016

11:40 a.m.

No calls this morning. Went to clinical supervision for my job.

Having a hard time breathing. Bill told me Bryan won't have a phone for a week. I go to Florida in ten days.

Will I be able to see him?

Will he leave this program?

Three places in three weeks...

What do I tell family?

People don't really understand. I hear tone and judgment in people's voices when I talk to them. Then there are stretches of silence – I hate it.

Worried, stressed. I am having difficulty concentrating, feeling like crying any second; can't cry yet.

8:41 p.m.

He called from Detox/stabilization. "I will not be able to call again for a few days. I went by a place that I used to use, but because you are coming down in a week, I didn't want to use."

That doesn't entirely make me feel better... still feeling anxious and worried...trying to breathe...

September 9, 2016

I worked. Had appointments for most of the day. I called the State's Attorney's office and tried to connect to complain about the last sober house that had their license revoked. I also talked to the President of FARR (Florida Association of Recovery Residences). He (they) are working with the task force to close down some of the illegal places.

I felt empowered and invigorated that maybe if I could help make a difference by reporting this stuff, it could make a difference for other addicts and their families.

NOTHING

Saturday September 10, 2016

Stephen and I did a bike ride – in preparation for our fundraiser, Cycle for Addiction Awareness next year.

We then watched the *20/20* special about Elizabeth Vargas, who is an alcoholic. I cried; I want to be telling a story of hope – I don't know if we will have that.

We participated in an addiction memorial event – more people came than last year – the media came again; it was a good evening.

NOTHING

Sunday September 11, 2016

Watched Netflix in the morning and baked cookies and granola.

Stephen and I did some work preparing to have our taxes reviewed.

Talked to Heather. Worked in my office some.

I think about Bryan always – felt a little guilty today because I felt relaxed and a little less stressed.

I still feel anxious about how the time in Florida will be. One week from today and I will be there.

NOTHING

Monday September 12, 2016

I did some work in the morning. Went on a two-hour bike ride. Lunch with Stephen, then showered and got ready to go to appointment for taxes.

Tax appointment at 3:00 –

I got a phone call from Bryan just after we got there.

I told him I was in an appointment and would call him after. No mention of leaving the detox or anything about the program or where he was.

2:06 p.m. – text from Bill

"Bryan got out of detox stabilization. He was supposed to go into a halfway house, but they told him that the beds were full. They put him on the streets in West Palm Beach, I just don't understand how he thinks this is ok."

"Mom, we got a call from Becky's Dr. – they want to talk to her about the results."

He called while I was in the store. He said that they gave him a Klonopin and Subutex as they were leaving.

He talked about detox like they were all bad people...I didn't know what to believe.

I talked to him about 4:15 p.m. He sounded a little slurry – he said he was trying to get hold of someone to get somewhere.

I went to a Naranon meeting, Thank God. It was me, Stephen, and another woman. It was helpful.

I talked to him after the meeting – he sounded worse.

"Mom, I gotta get help with my trauma. When I look in the mirror I see lifeless people, all my friends who I've seen dead. I'm so sorry, Mom, I want to see you happy and proud of me, (sobbing), I'm so sorry I can't stand it."

He told me he had started writing rap and it was helping him... to get it all out.

7:25 p.m.

"These dealers don't know they be taking these lives,

Heroin's killing kids, husband and wives."

"I'm really into this writing music and I know you don't like rap but I think I could be really, really good.

Where is he?

What is really going on?

Is he high?

8:40

"Where are you now?"

"Eating at Burger King. Going to Halfway soon."

Haalfwat

Where???

Halfway

I'm shaking sorry

Landaba

Landaba??

Nothing more…:(

11:19 p.m.

Bill texted: "Bryan returned to the detox facility, messed up – from Ted, a marketer/friend:

"Hi Mr. Massey, my name is Ted, Bryan wanted me to message you and let you know that him and Becky are ok and they are in detox until Monday or Tuesday at the latest."

Bill: "Bryan lied to you about what happened, they were supposed to go into PHP this morning, but they wanted to go to Halfway house and the facility said they weren't ready, and protocol had them going to separate PHP and then Halfway house in a month. He is really messed up, it's the second person that told me tonight he wasn't making any sense. His words were rambling, they had a hard time finding him, he was confused."

Me – awake until 1:00-ish

Will he live?

Should I bring him to Maine?

What will others say?

Is it enabling?

Can I help him?

Will I see him next week?

Will he die?

Should I plan a funeral?

Who should I call?

Where is everybody? I don't feel supported.

Oh yeah, everyone has their own children with addictions, and they can hardly stand it.

I don't want to tell Heather.

Tuesday September 13, 2016

7:37 a.m.

I called Vicky – the Admissions person where he had been.

She remembers him but she didn't work yesterday and didn't know if he came back.

She was understanding and explained their rules and program a bit. She said a counselor or someone would call me.

I had left a message yesterday for my doctor to get a prescription for Narcan....

Waiting

Waiting

Waiting

Can't breathe

What if the call is "'sorry, he was very sick, complications from all drug use – he is at the hospital, on life support.'"?

The other side says, "'Don't be so gloomy, he will pull out.

One day you will tell the stories,

There is hope,

Stay positive.

An hour later, Bill called and said they got kicked out of rehab – Becky had a syringe in her bag.

I had difficulty keeping up with this little daily journal. As I write this, it is 1 p.m. on Thursday, and I can hardly remember all that has happened.

Bryan and Becky went to the hospital. It turns out she had pneumonia. He has bronchitis. Bryan said he would be willing to go to a more reputable rehab if Becky could get set up somewhere.

I contacted Lenny – he told me to have Bryan call him and he did. They arranged for him to go.

I held my breath.

3:04 p.m.

Bill dropped Becky at the hospital; there was an argument and Bryan ended up at another hospital. She said she was pregnant, again, and Bryan was so upset he was going to leave the hospital.

3:56 p.m. – text

"Any updates from your Dr.'"

> "Yeah, bronchitis. I'm with Lenny now. I'm here.
> At the Rehab. And got antibiotic. Beck is pregnant."

"Ok, take it all one step at a time…"

> "She is blaming me for everything…"

"She is unwell. She cannot see straight right now. Hang in there."

> "'I'm hurt."

"'I know…. she needs time to get help and so do you. . So much pain and confusion in this disease.'"

> "Yeah, I know."

"Are you going to detox?"

> "Yes. The heroin is so strong that I get so sick."

"'I am so glad you are alive. Keep fighting and I will too."

To Bill:

"Try to enjoy your evening…I will try too." " He said, "I am bowling now."

10:56 p.m. text from Bill

"You awake?"

I was not.

Wednesday September 14, 2016

6:17 a.m. – Me to Bill:

"Sorry I was not up, everything ok?"

I talked to Peggy at the rehab, and she handles prescription information and talked some about the program.

Bryan sounded good; I was able to talk to him a bit.

From Bill:

"Bryan is going to leave rehab because of Becky. She
left the hospital, and he thinks she will
die without him. He called Becky."

4:42 p.m.

"What??!! I just talked to Peggy an hour ago."

I talked to Bryan; he just wanted to make sure Becky is safe somewhere – we talked a little about her lack of willingness to accept help.

By 7:00 p.m. – It was clear that Bryan had stayed at the rehab. He said he didn't want to jeopardize his legal issue (a pending legal charge). And I am going down on Sunday, and I think that was a consideration.

-Breathing slightly easier – Continued thoughts of:

Will he stay?

Should he come north?

How long will we all be doing this?

Will he be able to stay in Florida?

Will he live?

Thursday September 15, 2016

7:54 a.m. – To Bill:

"FYI, I talked to Bryan last night. He is staying, just worried about Becky dying…"

8:08 a.m.

"Becky is in St. Mary's hospital in Stuart with pneumonia again."

"I do hope she accepts help – she has refused a lot of offers."

10:10 a.m.

"Mom, I just wanted to let you know
my charges got dropped."

He had called a little earlier with his counselor to schedule an appointment for next week when I am down there.

I picked up my Narcan prescription today…. what if I have to use it? The reason for needing to scares the hell out of me.

By 9 p.m., he had left the rehab, then realized he made a mistake and wanted to go back. Becky was offered places, and she wouldn't go.

Friday September 16, 2016

I woke up at 2 a.m. and couldn't go back to sleep…five appointments scheduled for work.

9:56 a.m. – Bill sent me a text from a guy who owns the HWH; he gave me his contact information.

He had an option to go back to the rehab – he said he was going to call sometime during the day. .

By 9:25 p.m.

"I don't even know what to say, I'm so embarrassed
and upset with myself. I just don't know what to say."

"Did you get your stuff yet from the rehab?"

"I'm on my way to Port St. Lucie just not where everyone wants me to go or where's the best. I want to get well too, I really do."

"Where are you going? Why would you not go where is best? I don't understand…"

"We are going to a different rehab. I'm gonna
figure it out and make it right…"

I had a conversation with the HWH guy – he said I couldn't talk to Bryan but I could come visit. He tried to convince me it was a good place – HWH would be paid by Insurance through IOP.

Illegal!!!

Saturday September 17, 2016

Left at 6 a.m. to go to Massachusetts. Met up with Heather and Jeff at Beth's and visited with the baby. Went to the cemetery and took a picture of two of Bryan's friends who are there due to drug overdose. Went to visit with my mom and took my sister out to dinner and for ice cream for her birthday. I was completely exhausted. I cried during much of the car ride down to Massachusetts. The anticipation of seeing Bryan, very sad about all his challenges. I just couldn't stop crying. I have never felt like this before…it's horrible. And no one knows what to say – so often, they say nothing. That is almost worse!

Sunday September 18, 2016

I landed in Florida about 11:15 a.m.

I met up with Catherine. She called someone she knew who knew what house Bryan and Becky were at.

Before that, I had called the house manager/owner of the program, I honestly don't know his title. He was an asshole. He wasn't going to let me see Bryan, not going to tell me where he was, and he yelled at me. I yelled back – I'm his mother and that supersedes any title he has!

We got to the HWH, and Bryan came out and gave me a big, huge hug. He went in and got his stuff; he literally had only a handful.

Becky ended up coming with us – he asked if we could get her somewhere safe. It was not clear to any of us what would happen – who was going where.

I wanted them in separate treatment centers. We went to lunch. During lunch, it came out that Becky wanted to go home to California. Catherine worked on a plane ticket for her.

We went to Bill's to get her birth certificate and we went to a second time for Bryan to get more clothes.

Becky went to the airport. Bryan refused to go anywhere by himself and wanted to stay with her.

We had gone to the rehab to get the rest of her stuff and he had left there. They didn't have his stuff. I think they just thought he would be staying there.

There were high emotions throughout the day, and everyone was feeling it. We were all upset for our own reasons, crying, frustration, confusion, disappointment, and biggest of all, fear.

I had been awake since 3:00 a.m. and got back to the hotel about 9:00 p.m. without Bryan – I was so sad and scared, I left him and Becky at the airport.

Monday September 19, 2016

Bryan and Becky ended up at different sober houses – he said he was going back to a program he had been at before. It was an IOP program. I picked him up at about 9:00. We went to try to get his stuff from the rehab. They gave him his stuff but no medications. He had been diagnosed with bronchitis, but they threw out all the meds including antibiotic.

I dropped him back off because I had a meeting with some folks about a task force. I ate a small salad and cried every time I tried to talk. I was embarrassed but I was just so exhausted and scared and having someone who understood listen brought me to tears.

He was supposed to do his intake for a program, but the person didn't show up.

The intake was done before dinner, and I met the owner.

I went back to the hotel and didn't catch up with Bryan again until later. I got to rest a little which I probably needed. We went to dinner. He said that the night before there had been a big fight between a couple who were staying there; they were using, the police came, pounding on the door.

That didn't make me feel really good about them staying there.

We had a nice visit, talked about addiction, his process, why he didn't want to leave Becky (she doesn't have any idea of moderation). He says he uses more to not be sick – but then why does he go back to using after being clean? I didn't ask, but wonder.

We ate dinner at Duffy's, he brought some food to Becky.

I dropped him back off – had to pick up Becky because she had been out wandering while we were at dinner.

I felt bad.

Tuesday September 20, 2016

Noah's five-year anniversary of dying.

I picked Bryan and Becky up about 8:40 a.m. – Bryan came out of the house crying – it was a long night, for him – he didn't sleep. He cried, we hugged – we got in the car – listened to "I Drank a Beer" and started talking about Noah. We saw a dog and it was like one Noah used to have.

We went to Dunkin Donuts and talked and looked at pictures.

We held hands and all made a commitment for the future.

We went to the park to do our 'celebration' for Noah.

Bryan fed a squirrel, and it ate out of his hand! He said it was Noah, visiting him.

> "Mom, I'm gonna stay here at least 30 days – then we'll see. I want to see you in December. I really want to stop living like this. I'm glad the driver picked us up when he did; I might not have gone."

Wednesday September 21, 2016

I felt exhausted, relieved, slightly fearful of the future – will he live? I have a life, other kids. I went to a SMART meeting in the evening.

I had a 9:00 appointment and got a few work things done.

Laundry, unpacked.

I called the last treatment center Bryan had been at – he never got his remaining medications, especially penicillin. There was no answer and no return call. I was not happy!

NOTHING

Thursday September 22, 2016

I had a strong realization of how sick I had been getting. It takes enormous mental and emotional strength to endure this experience. I'm so glad I got to see him – It ended up being a 'great' weekend – I felt connected to him – we laughed, cried, and reminisced; there was hope. If I don't see him again – it would be a good last visit.

Who thinks like that?!

I called his program twice, left messages. I was told that he would call with his counselor…nothing. I was pissed, concerned, frustrated….

Is this really a good place?

NOTHING

Friday September 23, 2016

I had six clients today, I was exhausted. During the day, I got to connect with the clinical director at the treatment program Bryan is at. I told her I had called the counselor, with no return call, and that I had been told by her that the counselor would call me. I said that it has been very difficult to know who to trust and scary with their (Bryan and Becky) running around.

She told me he is doing fine; he is attending groups and that doesn't usually happen in detox. He looks forward to football on the weekend. I felt relieved, reassured, and grateful for her response.

NOTHING

Saturday September 24, 2016

Did some shopping at Sam's Club.

Walked the dogs.

Dinner with Heather and Jeff.

Talked with Jeff about some recovery stuff. He shared some recent experiences with his sponsor, and we talked about healthy behaviors vs. unhealthy ones.

NOTHING

Sunday September 25, 2016

Stephen and I went on a two-hour hike in the morning.

My sister called to check in about the trip I took to Florida.

Stephen and I watched a movie in the evening.

NOTHING

Monday September 26, 2016

Stephen and I went on a 15-mile bike ride.

Heather and I went shopping – got some much-needed items for myself – rain gear and a pair of hiking pants that fit.

Naranon meeting – it was very good!

NOTHING

Tuesday September 27, 2016

I had an appointment in the morning with a client who has a child who struggles with addiction.

I talked to Bryan and his counselor. It was a full hour – way more than other programs have offered.

She listened a lot, interjected some, offered Bryan some good support and suggestions for treatment.

> "I have a lot of questions about things that happened when I was a kid.

I'm going to commit to staying for at least 30 days. It's a small program so I can see the counselor almost as much as I want. I really don't want to keep living this way, for myself or my family.

I noticed that I was hopeful and happy about the interaction but felt like I wanted to moderate it to avoid future disappointment. These are big questions and serious issues.

> "I want to know why we went away to the Cape
> when I was little. I didn't understand. What
> was going on? How did Uncle Peter die?
> They always asked me about suicide."

Still, happy, content, and grateful for today.

Wednesday September 28, 2016

Walked the dogs in the morning.

Had four appointments during the day.

I was practically skipping – happy, and aware of the strong connection between Bryan's well-being and my happiness.

Codependence?

NOTHING

Thursday September 29, 2016

Stephen and I walked the dogs, then bike ride of ten miles.

I went and did a consultation with a peer about EMDR.

I talked with my friend whose daughter is here from Connecticut – I gave her some contact info re: NA for her.

I called a counselor to try to schedule a conference call with her and Bryan for next week.

It's still hard wondering how Bryan is. I know a mom who doesn't talk to her daughter and is very happy. She tells everyone that. Sometimes I feel guilty when I don't want to know all his pain. But I don't want to not talk to him…. that would not make me happy in any way.

NOTHING

Friday September 30, 2016

I called the counselor again to try to schedule for next week. No answer, no call back. I called Bill – he has heard from the facility to schedule another appointment.

She (the counselor) sent him (Bill) a Facebook friend request... what???!!

Some panic, fear, and uncertainty set in.

He is still there as far as I know...that's the only saving grace right now.

NOTHING

October 2016

Saturday, October 1, 2016

We went to a holistic fair from 10-4 and Stephen had a Reiki table set up. We met a lot of great people and enjoyed the day.

We had dinner with Heather and Jeff to celebrate her getting a new job. Stephen and I came home and had a fire in the fire pit and did a manifesting New Moon meditation.

Feeling blessed today with so many good things in this life.

NOTHING

Sunday October 2, 2016

I decided to begin an eight-week mindfulness online course.

Stephen and I went for a hike today and then rested and watched TV for the rest of the day.

I still feel anxious about how Bryan is – no news is good news?

I miss hearing his voice; I hope he is doing well. Tomorrow is Monday and maybe I'll hear something.

I think about what it is like for moms who will never talk to their son or daughter again. It is such a painful thought…I pray I don't have to know that reality.

I texted with a dad who also has a child addicted to heroin. We hadn't texted in a long time – I cried…. we all struggle.

NOTHING

Monday October 3, 2016

I woke up and did a body scan, part of the mindfulness program.

I walked the dogs, did paperwork in the office.

I got a message, but my phone never rang: "Hi Mom – I don't know
if I'll have a chance to call again, I'm doing good. I will try again."

Then I called the rehab where he was – I wanted to find out about
our phone session with the counselor.

There was no answer at a couple of numbers – finally a counselor
called and said she doesn't work on Fridays and had just gotten in.
I apologized for being a pest. I just felt so anxious and desperate
to know something!

I went down to the water with a friend and her daughter. Heather
and Jeff stopped by just after my friends left. Then Bryan called...

> "Hi Mom. I'm doing ok. I am still committed to
> staying for 30 days. I know we 'meet' tomorrow
> with Kimberly. I have to think what to talk about."

Tuesday October 4, 2016

I had that phone conference with Kimberly and Bryan. Ground
rules were set. After each one talks, the other has to repeat what
they heard.

It was a full hour of discussion about how things have been, why
and what we can do going forward. I started crying a little when
Bryan said this:

> "I want to set some boundaries, but I don't want to
> hurt anyone's feelings. I need to be more comfortable
> talking to other people and finding my own solutions
> to problems and not lean on you so much. I don't
> want you to take this the wrong way."

...but some of my tears were about relief and happiness that it
was progress. Some may have been upset about their child not
needing them as much – and I talked about that and how I have

worked on that in therapy. I guess I had a mix of emotions, letting go and holding on seem to be a constant challenge.

Wednesday October 5, 2016

Hurricane Matthew is coming to Florida. I am scared, won't be able to have contact probably. 130 mph winds expected.

10:00 a.m. – spoke briefly – was 'reassured' that the residents would be kept safe – they may be able to call Friday. Also, will connect next week with the new counselor.

I saw five clients throughout the day and was able to maintain focus.

Thursday October 6, 2016

One client in the morning.

My emotions were all over – worried about the storm, their emotional safety as well as physical safety.

The storm is supposed to be the strongest tonight and no one (my family) has called to check up on me or Bryan, or my brother who is in Florida.

RESENTMENT

FEAR

WORRY

3:30 p.m. went for a 16-mile bike ride with Stephen.

NOTHING

Friday October 7, 2016

My stepmother called this morning; we talked while I was on my way to work. We had a good talk.

She said she didn't know what to say to Bryan, but she thinks about him always. I told her to say that. Her boyfriend is 35 years in AA; "Maybe I should learn more," she said.

My mother texted, 1:30 p.m. and asked about Bill (my ex) and Anthony (my brother), both of whom are in Florida, both of whom she doesn't like, and I am not close with either, but she did not ask about Bryan.

My sister called at 7:30 p.m. and asked about "The Family in Florida." I texted back a short text....she didn't say any names, it felt very distant.

I'm hating the family thing and worried about Bryan.

NOTHING

Saturday October 8, 2016

I went to the counselor's today in the a.m. to help get my head 'straight.' I called my mother and sister and thanked them for checking in...they did do that, so I have to remember that. I struggle with resentments and continue to work on it in meetings and in therapy.

Stephen and I went kayaking and went to the Belgrade Harvest Festival. We ate lunch and I wrote notes. I am still feeling really frustrated not hearing from Bryan.

Finally, at 5:30 p.m. I called Peggy; she got a message to Bryan to call – he DID!

> "Hi Mom! Not much happened here, didn't you
> see the news? I'm good. I was disappointed about
> the storm. I will call you Tuesday, maybe Wednesday
> with my new counselor. Can you ask
> Dad to bring my food stamps?"

All my worry.... the storm did not hit his area very hard.

Sunday October 9, 2016

I did my mindfulness practice, and Stephen and I went hiking.

I talked some about my inner struggles regarding my family. Trying to think of the Buddhist practice – it is what it is....not in the cliché way, but in the acceptance of reality way.

Stephen and I started talking about doing a fundraising bike ride for addiction awareness.

NOTHING

Monday October 10, 2016

Stephen and I started out to do a training bike ride; we had planned to ride north and camp overnight. We only rode ten miles total due to the cold rain. It didn't feel safe, and it was going to be 50 miles. We turned around and it rained most of the day. We went and saw Heather for a bit and brought her some food. She had been going to watch our dogs.

We talked about family addiction and Bryan.

NOTHING

Tuesday October 11, 2016

I did my morning meditation and then I had four client appointments, one of whom is also a mother of an addict.

I got a text from Bryan; he was with his dad
and asked me to call him.

I went shopping with Heather and out to lunch. It was a nice day and I enjoyed very little guilt.

He said that he was doing well, and they were out to
lunch and had had a session with the counselor.

I asked questions; he answered them but with not a lot of detail.

"I'm going to start talking about where to go next
– the guy who does that is good and knows a lot of
people. I'll have my counselor call you."

I feel anxious – will he be able to make a good decision? It seems like he has done well, will that end?

I went to a friend's house for a visit; it was relaxing and enjoyable. I was reminded to put faith in the process and Bryan and also myself.

55

Wednesday October 12, 2016

I did my morning meditation and had some appointments as well as work in the office. I walked the dogs twice.

I went to the see the house in New Sharon with Heather and Jeff that they are interested in buying.

Bill called during that appointment, "I'm worried about Bryan – did you know that he sold his X-Box while you were here and was high the whole time?"

I felt anxious and worried and had to 'snap out of it' and return to the present and the fact that it is 'out of my control.'

I went to a SMART recovery meeting and shared about being proud of him being there for three weeks and cried.

NOTHING

Thursday October 13, 2016

I was supposed to talk with Bryan's counselor (the new one) this week. She didn't call.

I had difficulty managing anxiety not knowing how things are going.

I talked to the counselor for about 20 minutes, then we had a brief call together with Bryan. I felt so much better.

> "I have some things to figure out – but I'm doing it. I don't know about Becky – I don't think she has been honest, and I don't know what to believe. She acts like a child a lot. I will call you tomorrow, trying not to talk to dad as much."

Friday October 14, 2016

I felt better going to work after talking to Bryan – but worry a little about him going to a safe HWH, how he feels about staying in treatment longer.

I called and talked with his case manager, Ryan, and said that I wanted to extend the suggestion that if he can't find good housing could he come to Maine for a break and safe place and do research from here. He said he would pass it on at the team meeting and have him call that night."

I worked and felt good, not worried.

I had two new clients who did not realize how they have been affected by another's drinking and using – it sounded strange to them.

8:15 p.m.

> "Hi Mom. We went to a meeting, and we are going to eat now. I am not talking to Dad much – let him know how I am, and I will call you Monday."

Saturday October 15, 2016

I rested a lot today.

I am working on myself – trying to put my faith and trust in Bryan, God, whoever, that he will be ok and make good choices for himself.

NOTHING

Sunday October 16, 2016

Stephen and I participated in another Holistic Fair. It was amazing and there was great energy there!

I went to a workshop with a spiritual medium

And I was called on first. "Grandmother, you are a lot alike – she is proud of you. She is around. The last three to four months. You have been feeling alone – she and others are with you – she wants you to feel this love." I cried – was tired after then and talked to Heather some – I felt better.

Stephen and I did a full moon ritual – releasing the old and unhelpful situations and energy and drawing in good and new and helpful.

NOTHING

Monday October 17, 2016

Mostly a quiet day.

> He said he was going to call Monday....

This was my first day on Weight Watchers. I have gained almost 20 pounds over the past year or so. Did a mindfulness practice and did a yoga practice – felt good.

I did some work and rested, showered, grocery shopped then...

> NOTHING until...

> 3:15 p.m. – Bill

> "Bryan called and then he hung up on me, I was talking about his next move...he got mad at me and hung up. We talked about Maine and what are the plans as far as him and Becky...The clinical director called and said that something happened on Saturday..."

6:27 p.m.

"I think Bryan and Becky are trying to leave because on Wednesday or Thursday, she gets money on her food stamps so they can sell it to get high."

SAD – SCARED – DISAPPOINTED - CONFUSED

Thursday October 18, 2016

I woke up and was crying by 6:00 a.m. I want this pain and struggle to end...for us all – it feels like no way for that to happen...

10:00 a.m.

I called for the scheduled counselor call – Bryan sounded okay but a little anxious about leaving – there was discussion about when his actual 'time was up.'

> "Hi Mom. How are you?"

"Well, ok…"

"Why? What's going on?"

I expressed my concerns about what I heard from his father – we talked about addiction and trust. He doesn't trust some of the people he encounters –

"I am leaving tomorrow, and they may make it be AMA because I'm not going to their referral – it's all about their referral/business and I don't give a fuck about that – this is my life!"

We had some discussion about whether or not detox counts, over an hour we were on the phone…concerns were expressed about him and Becky – bottom line: from his perspective, it's basic needs – he has insurance, that can help get them housing; she has food stamps, gets them food.

I called the owner at the HWH.

Wednesday October 19, 2016

Plans were made for them to go to HWH – at first it was going to be 10 a.m. then 3 p.m.

I had a canceled a.m. client appointment and did some exercise in the morning then four client appointments – it was a good day overall.

7:56 p.m.

"On the way to HWH"

A little anticipation in his voice.

Slight anxiety over Bryan going to HWH – anticipation, will he be ready? How will it be with Becky?

10:06 p.m. – text from Bryan to Becky

"I'm not playing your mind games you don't care about my feelings or well anything but yourself.

59

You left me. But you love me?
You left to get a needle I hope it was worth it."

Thursday October 20, 2016

I had a counselor appointment in the morning, good appointment, I felt really good about how I'm doing despite some anxiety – staying focused on me. Client appointment, then dentist appointment.

7:06 a.m.

"I can't sleep anymore; I always wake up at 6:00. Dad's gonna bring me shoes today."

Client appointment at 3:30 p.m., it was good. Just as it ended, Bill called.

I didn't answer – don't want to feed into fear – he texted, "It's not good."

I called Bryan at 4:50 p.m. – No answer

I walked the dogs, called him.

"Bryan and Becky walked away from the HWH. Bryan turned up at the house naked and screaming and swearing at every one – out of his mind. They took him away in the ambulance." I talked to Bryan in the hospital at 10 p.m. "Mom, I'm going to a program after this." I talked to the program manager throughout the evening – they got him to the program late Thursday night.

11:17 p.m.

"I'm scared for Becky."

That was his concern…Becky.

Friday October 21, 2016

The HWH, police, and Bill had tracked Becky down and escorted her to the airport and put her on a plane back to California.

Calls throughout the day – Bryan arrived late Thursday and said…

"Mom, I had to leave. If I stayed there, I was going to die.
I am worried about Becky. Can you let me
know if you hear anything?"

By the end of the day, it was confirmed that she was on a plane home to California. According to Bill, she was going to turn herself in on a warrant.

I did – I let him know that I heard she was going back to California.

By evening I was so happy – feeling like there was a chance for Bryan to focus fully on himself.

Saturday October 22, 2016

** A lost day…just getting through**

Sunday October 23, 2016

I have been so stressed – wondering how he was doing. I felt better seeing he was on Facebook, being able to let him know he is not alone, that I believe in him.

8:21 a.m. on FB

Me: "Hey! Miss you so much!"

Bryan: "Love and miss you too, still no sleep.
I have a cold sore and I'm struggling mentally"

Me: "Any way to call? I'm sending positive vibes."

Bryan: "No, not today – tomorrow
I'll call. I am hurting."

Me: "Hang in there, it will pass…with time. I booked a trip – talk to you tomorrow."

Bryan: "Ok. Where are you seeing me and when?"

Me: "We will talk about it."

Bryan: "Ok, I love you."

I finished work for my work and walked the dogs.

I spent the afternoon with Stephen catching up on TV shows.

As evening came, I felt a little more uneasy – anxiety setting in again, uggghh!

Monday October 24, 2016

Stephen went to Massachusetts for the week – work and a Reiki class and to see his kids.

9:48 a.m.

Bryan said he would be going somewhere that night
– he said he was going to "look into his options."
He started out saying he was going to Phoenix,
then maybe California – even though he swore it
wasn't because Becky is there – he said he
"needs to get out of South Florida."

I walked the dogs and prepared myself for the week – feeling anxious. By noon, they were on the road, Bill didn't know what to do.

3:00 p.m.

"I miss Becky. I know everyone thinks it's other stuff
than the fact that she's my best friend and we got so
close, and I was so happy in treatment with everything,
and I have my parents who my decisions
expect so greatly. The pain has been enough."

The conversation went downhill. I offered him to come to Maine – and I could help him get into a program in Massachusetts and he will be closer to family. I just wanted to try to understand his rationale.

He stopped responding to me – wouldn't answer texts – made me feel more anxious.

I went to my Naranon meeting that night; it was me and one other person, and it was great to be there.

9:53 p.m.

"Working on treatment."

"Please come north – just consider it."

"Yes, ok. I love you. I feel horrible;
I have a terrible headache."

Tuesday October 25, 2016

Bryan said he had treatment lined up – in California.

9:45 a.m.

In the morning, we argued about what he was doing and why. I did not get an explanation that made sense – he stammered and was not giving a straight answer. We hung up.

Bill: "I gave up a long time ago trying to change Bryan's mind; he thinks he always knows best and won't listen to reason. I am just tired of it all"

Bill sent a link to where Bryan was going.

2:30 p.m.

Bryan: "Boarding the flight now.
I love you Mother so much."

Me: "I love you so much. Safe travels. I talked to
the admissions guy; he filled me in on what to
expect. Maybe I'll come for family week. Keep
moving forward, stay strong and I love you! No matter
what, I love you. No matter what
I love you – no matter what!!"

I was so hopeful and felt more confident about where he was going, even though it was so far away. The admission people do a good job at reassuring us moms…provide hope. My confidence and hope soar.

4:31 a.m.

"I'm here at the treatment center. (It was a different
one than he said he was going to.) I'll call you
tomorrow afternoon. Long story with the other place.
I'm clean like I said and didn't need detox. I love you.
I'm safe and staying here 60 maybe 90 days. I love you
so much and have hope. We will make it
through this I promise you. I love you."

Wednesday October 26, 2016

I did yoga in the morning and then a walk. Prepared for five client
appointments. Full day of work.

1:30 p.m.

I got a call from the first place that Bryan never got picked up by
them – he wasn't at the airport. At that time, I didn't know what
was going on.

1:47 p.m.

Doing intake now.

Where?!

He named the recovery center.

2:57 p.m.

He sent me a picture of the place that he was at, with a view of
ocean in the background.

3:09 p.m.

"I tried to call – I'm turning my phone over now."

Thursday October 27, 2016

I went for a walk in the morning and then had a 9:00 appointment.

I spent an hour on the phone with the first place he had planned
to go to.

Did grocery shopping and walked the dogs. While we were out, a loose dog came after us. Someone called the police, and they told them that someone got bit by a dog; that wasn't the case, but I was screaming, and it was a stressful situation.

I was exhausted after this…it felt like too much. But I have to work – I feel like a fraud.

NOTHING

Friday October 28, 2016

I did yoga and had an 8:45 appointment.

Five appointments scheduled for the day.

Laundry in the middle of the day at a laundromat.

Bryan happened to call while I was there. He said that his phone calls have to be short from here. He got really upset – he said nothing happened but there aren't any counselors there. He said he is good and that all is going well. Becky's mom is going to visit, and she is going to meet him. He asked if I was going to come out – I still feel betrayed and not really ready to spend that money.

Saturday October 29, 2016

I went for a walk with the dogs in the morning.

Went to a psychic fair with a friend in the afternoon…it was nice!

NOTHING

Sunday October 30, 2016

10:46 a.m.

"Are you awake or is someone else on your FB?"

11:00 a.m.

"I'm awake Mother, how are you?"

(I interpret his use of the word, "Mother," as a word he uses when high or under influence of something. I don't know if he knows that or even if it's true, but I have a reaction to it.)

12:50 p.m.

The phone rings, a call from Bryan. I didn't hear much, then Bryan got a little loud – I couldn't really understand. Afraid he butt-dialed and was using.

> Then he said, "Stay on the phone and
> record this conversation seriously, please"

He sounded really anxious and upset. I guess someone pulled his arm and wasn't respectful to Becky. He was slurring.

> "These guys are assholes – I wanted to stab him.
> I said I wanted to leave."

He sounded crazed...I could only guess at what was happening on the other end of the phone. I don't even know if what I thought was an accurate guess – I was just left with a lot of my own imagination. I didn't want to be in my head.

5:31 p.m.

I finally got to talk the clinical director. We talked about his behavior and medications.

From Bill:

"Bryan is walking the streets now. He left. Becky is with him, both left, both out of their minds. I gave them a number to get help. The clinical director gave it to me."

Me: "ok...we keep praying..."

Bill: "He told me he's going to kill himself. He wants me to get him a room. I told him no and gave him a number to get help."

He wanted Bill to fly him back to Florida. He called me twice; I was in the bathroom and didn't answer.

He called me again about 9:15 p.m.; said he was going back to detox.

Bill: "Bryan is going to one of the places that the clinical director recommended, and she said it is up to him. I guess Becky is going to a different place."

NOTHING

Monday October 31, 2016

I walked the dogs for an hour.

Just letting Bryan BE....

I talked to the clinical director for a bit – we talked about Bryan and the placement and the plan. He is in Santa Ana and Becky is in Anaheim.

I scheduled a vacation for Stephen and me to take. I told him we need a few days to be away from the house – and day to day stuff. We will shop and sleep and eat and relax for four nights. We have not done that in a long, long time.

I need to live my life regardless of what happens to him.... it's a daily challenge for me. I am fighting daily to survive this.

NOTHING

November 2016

Tuesday November 1, 2016

I did an hour walk with dogs in the morning then did some work for work.

I talked to Bryan's counselor – wanted him to get a message. We are here for you – fighting with you as long as it takes.

He is still in detox – they are beginning to talk about next steps – it seems he still wants to try HWH next – seems to want to rush the process or something… maybe doesn't think he's 'as bad' as others think.

5:43 p.m.

The clinical director called just to check in. She has been amazingly helpful and supportive, and I told her that her 'style' of talking to Bryan was perfect.

NOTHING

Wednesday November 2, 2016

I did a walk/run in the morning and a morning meditation.

I had four appointments during the day.

Bill checked in twice during the day – he seems to have a hard time not talking to Bryan.

I felt happy – a little guilty for being happy

happy….

NOTHING

Thursday November 3, 2016

I had a dentist appointment – root canal.

I spent the rest of the day with Stephen.

I talked to the clinical director at night – she reassured me he is safe and doing okay.

NOTHING

Friday November 4, 2016

I worked during the day.

Walked in the morning.

He called from the treatment program.

"Becky wanted me to come to her HWH, the manager said it was ok but I'm going to stay here. I'm gonna do what they tell me – I don't want to die."

I am always thinking about him – trying to keep my anxiety low – my balance and faith that no matter what happens we are okay.

Saturday November 5, 2016

I went walking and hiking and then shopping with Heather and Stephen. It was a long day but a good one.

I talked about Bryan a little – that he sounded like he was talking with some "change talk."

I felt encouraged.

NOTHING

Sunday November 6, 2016

I hung out with Stephen – caught up on shows. We rested and prepared for the week.

2:25 p.m.

"Hi Mom. I'm kind of bored and a little lonely,
but it's ok. Once the week starts it will get better."

Monday November 7, 2016

I worked in the office in the morning and walked the dogs twice during the day.

I got two new client appointment calls – yay! One is interested in group.

5:45 p.m.

I called the clinical director. "I spent most of the day
with him – he is down because he didn't get to see Becky."

Went with Heather and Jeff to look at a house. It is right down the street from us, and it is very exciting to think they may move there.

7:15 p.m.

He called – miserable.

"Why am I here? I have nothing to look forward to...
no family for Christmas, Becky has her family here....
I don't know what to do. I have no clothes left
– why do I feel like this?"

Went to Naranon meeting – no one showed up so went shopping and came home.

My anxiety skyrockets immediately...this is not a good sign. His drug brain is kicking in...

Tuesday November 8, 2016

I worked in the office and had two appointments in the afternoon.

I walked with Stephen in the afternoon.

> Talked to Bryan – he sounded much, much better.
> He said he went to a meeting and might have a
> sponsor. He hopes to see Becky tomorrow.

Went to bed early…. tired!

Wednesday November 9, 2016

I woke up a couple of times during the night – kept thinking about the vote.

I woke up at 3:45 a.m. and had to know…I was shocked!

Went for a walk in the morning with Stephen and did yoga.

I had three appointments in the afternoon.

Heather and Jeff negotiating on the house.

NOTHING

Thursday November 10, 2016

Facebook – "I love you so much"

9:55 a.m. – FB

"I love you mother"

I had supervision in the morning and three clients during the day, so it felt like a full day of work to me.

> "I just sent Heather a message – first time since I've
> been here – and she was so angry with me the last time
> we talked. I've been thinking about it ever since and
> I basically said I'd rather have you be angry at me for
> life over the choice I made that you didn't understand
> or agree with than have to bury me and
> live with that for the rest of your life."

It was shortly after the election, and I was still very upset about that.

Friday November 11, 2016

Six client appointments during the day.

Bryan texted in the morning – he got his phone back.

He said he would do his best to make his plan,
but if he didn't feel good about it, he wouldn't go.

I called the clinical director in the afternoon - she said they were having some challenges with Bryan but that they are working with him.

11:00 a.m. – Facebook

"If you get a chance, listen to 'Love Yourz' by J. Cole
– it says the N word, but ignore that and
listen to the message."

I said I might like to schedule a trip out there, but I didn't want Bryan to know ahead of time – the clinical director said we could work it out.

Bryan is going to see Becky – there will be an itinerary that he will have to follow or there will be consequences. I felt anxious and worried.

Saturday November 12, 2016

I walked the dogs, had coffee with a friend and her friend. I walked at the golf course for an hour and a half. I did some work for my job.

He picked up $25 that I had sent him through
Western Union – he had plans to go out with Becky
– they were going to the movies. It was to be a
six-hour pass and he was going to be taking a bus.

I felt anxious about this plan – Patty had said they had some concerns about his behavior.

I received a text, at 12:00 a.m., "I love you a ton Mom."

Sunday November 13, 2016

I walked the dogs early for a half hour. Left the house at 7 a.m. for Massachusetts.

Had lunch with my mother, sister, nephew, and his girlfriend. It was a nice visit – just long enough.

Had dinner with Beth, Alec, and Ana (Beth's daughter); Carl (Beth's boyfriend) backed out but we had a nice visit.

> 8:50 p.m. – He called and sounded good, no meds, wanted me to know he is ok – he wants time to process it all before talking to me about it. "Sorry for the worry" – he realized some things he could have done different.

I did not hear from Bryan all day – I tried to text, call, but the phone went right to voicemail. I called the house, left a message, and called the clinical director and left a message.

> By 9:00 p.m. I got a message from the clinical director that she had wanted Bryan to call me. She did not say much – he is in stabilization.

How can I keep feeling so split with enjoying time with those I am with and worrying and not knowing how or where he is?! How did things change so fast? This is why I can never relax.

Monday November 14, 2016

I woke up at 5:00 a.m., left the hotel, got coffee, and went up to the reservoir nearby to try to see the Super Moon set. We did not see it there – we saw the sun rise and hiked for 1.5 hours and then drove back to Maine.

> NOTHING

Went to Naranon – it was a great meeting, and the topic was about letting go.

> …back in detox/stabilization.

(Since Sunday night, a friend of his from back home who is in Florida went missing. Bryan was worried sick – by the afternoon, the kid was found.)

Tuesday November 15, 2016

I walked the dogs and had three client appointments that day. At 5:14 a.m., I texted, "Do you have your phone back?"

> 6:24 a.m. – "Yeah, I got it back and I can't sleep again. I'm beating myself up; I have had very bad anxiety."

"Try to rest – don't beat yourself up."

> "I know I can't. Becky, I think is leaving and idk just really sad stressed and confused."

8:14 a.m. "you're not sleeping…"

"Why is she leaving?"

> "stupid argument about a girlfriend messaging me"

He and Becky left the sober house they were in. No more clinical Director….Now in Laguna Beach.

Wednesday November 16, 2016

I had clients all day from 8:45 – 5.

> 9:23 a.m.

> "I love you. Have a great day."

It was a really good day – I loved the work with clients.

> 10:08 a.m. – He sent a Facebook memory, Run for Malawi. (that was a fundraising event he had been at)

Thursday November 17, 2016

> 10:20 a.m.

> "I love you Mom, sorry."

"Sorry?"

10:50 a.m.

"Why am I an addict, I don't understand?"

"I just feel like no matter what I do it's getting worse. I just don't know what to do anymore. I'm just mentally at a place I'm getting worse."

"I don't either – but you don't have to apologize. You can treat this and live a better life. I'm fighting with you and for you."

"I'm praying you get the answers you need to feel less stressed."

"I'm tryin. I'm scared."

I had a root canal in the morning and then went to Heather's to bring food – then had three appointments.

By the evening something happened, and they got kicked out of the sober house – dropped at Walmart. They were put up in hotel, got high, crack?!! Meth?!

Ugggghhh. Nothing I can do...

Friday November 18, 2016

I walked in the morning, early, then showered and my first two appointments canceled. I didn't see anyone until 12:00.

Throughout the morning, I was on the phone with Bryan, and George (the marketer). I was stressed, Bryan sounded awful, my clients were flaking out on me.

They got to the airport – late – they got an Uber set up by George. They went to get Becky's stuff first – the sober house didn't want to give it to her.

They missed the first flight and another one couldn't be booked until the next morning.

"I feel like I'm doing something wrong because we are handicapped."

TEXTS:

"Well…you are struggling that is for sure…I think you still struggle to understand your disease and treatment…"

They were trying to get Becky's stuff from the sober house, and no one was there to get it for them.

"This is miserable"

"Yep…move forward and into the life you deserve…ask Noah and Gampy for guidance. I am sending prayers and healing light your way."

"I know Gampy and Noah are watching over me…but I'm scared"

"I just feel I don't deserve it. I'm starving"

George (marketer) asked me to reimburse him for the flights that they missed. Ummmm…no, sorry. He was stressed by this also.

They missed the first flight and another one couldn't be booked until the next morning.

Saturday November 19, 2016

I woke up at 4:15 a.m.. Stephen and I walked for almost two hours at the golf course.

Not much conversation.

11:04 a.m.

"You on the plane?"

Nothing.

1:51 p.m.

"How about now?"

2:01 p.m. (they were in California)

"No, they pushed it back; I'll be on at 1:30"

Went to Farmington with Heather and Stephen. We got coffee and shopped. We had nachos out for lunch. It was real nice and relaxing.

According to Bill, Bryan and Becky fought
in the airport and caused scenes.

I got a text from George's mother: "I'm the mom of an addict, so I know what you are going through – you need to call him and tell him you love him…."

What???!!!

At one point during this time, Becky left but he stayed and wait-ed for the plane. We texted and he was so tired and rambling a bit. He wanted to follow her but knew it would cause problems with us if he didn't get on the plane. He continued to be worried about her and sounded really tortured by this whole situation.

Apparently, according to her, Bryan told her that I wasn't there for him…

Sunday November 20, 2016

12:54 a.m.

"I don't; I wasn't fit to fly"

1:20 a.m.

"What?! So where are you and what will you do now?"

11:33 a.m.

"so this is a new low for me…"

"I'm sorry"

"only one way to go… up…"

"Here's an offer: when you are READY to seriously work and change…come here, I can help you do that: therapy, job, struc-ture, doctors. When you are ready…do all that you can and need to…you deserve and can do way better than this. But you have to do it…"

"I know this has been hard I'm starting I'm scared I'm miserable"

"I love you very much"

"When you are ready, I am here."

"I love you very much...I believe you can figure it all out."

He and Becky had new plane tickets scheduled for 1:00 p.m. and would land on the east coast around 9:00 p.m.

I did a few notes in the morning for work.

I had a counselor appointment for me.

Stephen went shopping.

We relaxed on the couch for the afternoon.

9:44 p.m.

"We landed."

"Good.... hope all goes well the rest of the night. I love you and will talk to you when you can. Hope you get rest and feel better..."

Monday November 21, 2016

I slept a little better, a little later.

6:30 a.m.

Bryan called – said he slept a little. The time change made it difficult.

I worked in my office for three to four hours and Stephen did some work.

He slept at a HWH and would soon be at the detox.

I noticed a level of concentration (for me) that is different than the past few days... maybe a little clearer?

He called about 10:00 a.m. almost at the detox,
he wanted me to know that he loves me
and that he will call when he can.

I am feeling relieved that at least for a few days (Thanksgiving included) I know where he will be – as long as he stays. Teeny tiny hope.

I am trying to get my feet back under me.

Tuesday November 22, 2016

I worked in the morning.

Stephen cleaned.

NOTHING

Wednesday November 23, 2016

I worked in the morning.

Heather and Jeff came down about noon for Thanksgiving.

2:00 p.m.

Polly, "I am calling from 561-xxx-xxxx
– please call back."

"Is your son Bryan? Just had to check the
number. He will be calling later in the day."

We walked for about 45 minutes and then ate dinner.

We watched TV and had a real nice visit.

6:13 p.m.

Bryan called – he sounded tired, a little depressed.

"I just wanted to check in Mom, let you know I'm ok.
You were right, I tested positive for everything, except
pot and cocaine. I will call tomorrow on Thanksgiving."

Thursday November 24, 2016

Bill sent a text at 12:15 a.m. – "Bryan got kicked out of detox with Becky, I don't even know what to say."

I texted Bryan at 7:35 a.m. – asking where he was, called a couple times, no answer.

1:35 p.m.

He texted me, "Mom, the hospital lost my necklace you got me. :("

Stephen and I were just going for a walk – while out – calls started: George (marketer) trying to convince me to get Bryan to go where he wanted him to go. At one point he yelled at me into the phone, "If you don't want your son to die, you need to get him to go here or you are going to lose him."

I texted back and forth with Bill for much of the afternoon. Another detox and trying to figure out placement for another treatment center? Bill and I both feel at a loss…what's the answer? How do we help? At one point during this time, we texted about what we would do for a funeral…I had already thought about it and told him where it would be. It occurred to me then that that responsibility would probably be mine.

I was stressed and scared and confused; I didn't know what to believe or what I should do. I was also glad that we had celebrated Thanksgiving the day before, so the 'day' wasn't ruined…felt a little giddy about that.

Friday November 25, 2016

12:31 a.m. – "I'm here, I'll call you tomorrow I love you. This time I'm done."

I woke up about 5; I felt really tired.

I had four appointments scheduled and the first two no-showed. I am in a rented office space and not at home. The third client no-showed, and we were able to make other arrangements.

11:45 a.m.

I called the Detox – he signed a release, will call later with counselor.

Saturday November 26, 2016

I did notes in the morning and then drove to Belfast and went to the Alanon meeting there -it's an hour away.

He called from detox while we were at Alanon meeting. I called back and they said he was in group. It made me feel good to know where he was but felt upset that I had missed the call.

Went to lunch with Stephen. We did some shopping for Christmas. We drove back and watched Heather's dog.

Then had dinner.

Sunday November 27, 2016

I walked and ran in the morning then went to Heather's to help/ discuss packing.

I came back and showered.

I did Reiki with Stephen and then the group.

Had a counselor appointment at 6:30 p.m.

I felt good, but then often feel guilty for that.

NOTHING

Monday November 28, 2016

I cried in the morning; I have had a couple difficult night's sleeping. No word back from Bryan – don't know what's going on.

I called to check in with the counselor. They were able to put him on the phone. He had not gotten the message that I called the day before. He thought I was 'done' with him.

I had a real low energy day; Stephen said it was probably due to the Reiki attunement.

> He said, "I'm excited, excited for going to treatment."
> He also said he wanted to have some more distance
> – just so he can work on himself.

(Cautiously optimistic)

I felt better by the afternoon when Stephen got home…

I am ready for a full work week!

Tuesday November 29, 2016

I walked the dogs in the morning. It was freezing rain the rest of the day.

I had a few appointments today – last minute cancellation on the second to last appointment due to the weather. The last appointment no showed and no call. Her second cancel this week.

I thought about Bryan today – a little anxious because he goes to PHP tomorrow – praying, praying he makes changes – and that I can make the healthy changes too.

I ordered him another necklace to day – the third step prayer.

NOTHING

Wednesday November 30, 2016

I had six clients from 8:30 – 7:30 today.

It was a long day – but everyone showed, and I was happy!

I took the dogs for a walk in the middle of the day. Bill called; did I shut off insurance? They won't cover PHP. Bryan is going to a rehab in Port St. Lucie – Becky is going somewhere else.

"Hi Mom – I know you didn't shut off the insurance. It's the end of the year, it may renew in January. Sam is going to take me on scholarship. Becky is going somewhere else. I don't know – I just have to take care of myself right now. I love you."

I am anxious, hopeful – ugghhh, again.

December 2016

Thursday December 1, 2016

I did yoga, laundry, walked the dogs, and saw two clients, and did paperwork for work.

I had a productive day and also relaxed some during the day.

I was anxious to know how Bryan was doing and if he would call.

Looking forward to vacation. I booked a trip to Florida to surprise Bryan for Christmas, one overnight. I bought the insurance on the flight and also got free cancellation on the hotel reservation.

Live and learn…

NOTHING

Friday December 2, 2016

I worked in the office in Augusta. I had four appointments scheduled, three showed.

I walked on the golf course in the morning for an hour and a half.

I had a relaxing night with Stephen.

I called the rehab in Port St. Lucie to talk to the counselor, no one called back. :(Maybe next week – I want them to know I'm coming, but not him.

NOTHING

Saturday December 3, 2016

I ran a 5K with Heather; it was a trail run. I ran it two minutes faster than I have been running in recent races; pleasantly surprised. I credit it to doing yoga.

Went to look at Heather's new house and took pictures.

Went to a psychic fair. We talked to some people about various collaborative ideas; feeling excited!

NOTHING

Sunday December 4, 2016

I walked the dogs in the morning, packed up and went to Ogunquit – we are ON VACATION! We scheduled four days away. We were able to get there and unpack by 10:30 a.m. We did some shopping, ate lunch, walked on the beach, and ended the day with a nice beer watching the sun go down.

Becky texted – she left where she was and asked about Bryan. She said she was going to another program.

NOTHING

Monday December 5, 2016

It was our first full day of vacation, waking up here. Did a real nice walk, 'The Marginal Way.'

We went to breakfast and then relaxed at the room, watched some TV and napped.

I still feel a bit anxious about the 'not knowing' how Bryan is doing; especially knowing Becky is going somewhere else.

NOTHING

Tuesday December 6, 2016

Did a good meditation in the morning and then a yoga session.

Had breakfast, and left to go to Portsmouth, New Hampshire.

We did some shopping and got some Christmas gifts, went to lunch. Then we did some personal shopping and then went to see a lighthouse and a cliff walk.

> While we were out walking on the cliff walk, Bryan called – we talked for a few minutes, and he said he is struggling some but is determined to stay – a lot of emotions. He asked for money for cigarettes and said he is worried about Becky and Doug.

Wednesday December 7, 2016

Finished some shopping. Rested some more, last day of vacation. I feel a little guilty. NOT that I don't deserve it, but don't want him to feel bad.

> 4:10 p.m.

> He called and we talked briefly – he said he would call tomorrow.

Thursday December 8, 2016

Home from vacation.

I had appointments in the afternoon – settling back into our life.

I thought Bryan would call – maybe he called his dad instead of me. I told him it was ok if he felt he needed to call his dad, but I missed him today.

> 9:10 p.m.

> Two missed calls – I was already asleep. :(

Friday December 9, 2016

I had six appointments for work today.

I called Bryan's counselor in the afternoon – I had not received an email from her, also I wanted to know if I would hear from him – I wanted him to know I was asleep when he called. She and I connected and planned to do a conference call on Monday.

I told her I was still planning on the trip December 19th. She said he was doing good – he is 'willing'…what?! He was joining two groups.

I got new clients; that's exciting and one of them asked to get in to see me specifically that day; they have alcohol issues and cried during the first 20 minutes.

That made me happy.

Saturday December 10, 2016

I went for a walk with Stephen in the morning for one and a half hours. I drove to Connecticut to visit with a friend and to go to the play, *Wicked,* with her.

I had a nice visit with her and went to the play – we enjoyed it very much.

Bryan called at about 4:10 p.m. "I have a cold Mom – it has been cold here – 60 degrees." We laughed about the difference in temperature from Florida to Maine. He said he is good – playing poker. "I will call you on Monday. They want me to take this medication for ADD, but I don't want to take it – I don't want to be a guinea pig."

Sunday December 11, 2016

I went out to breakfast and then drove home – four hours from Connecticut.

I felt like I was getting a cold – was really tired and rested all afternoon, then went to sleep early.

NOTHING

Monday December 12, 2016

We had a snowstorm and appointments were canceled. I rested in the morning with Stephen.

I then did some work for work for a couple of hours and got files organized for the week.

We went to dinner with Heather and Jeff – one-year sober anniversary for Jeff. We bought him a necklace and gave him a card. He cried and was appreciative.

I wondered why Bryan didn't call – I hope all is ok for him. We had a good day, but… I wished I could have talked to him.

NOTHING

Tuesday December 13, 2016

I had five appointments during the day – it was a pretty good day.

Heather found out some stressful information about her house – the appraisal was not complete.

Bryan called in the evening. He still sounds good, said he is taking Naltrexone, is positive for Hep C and won't be able to start treatment for six months and then his insurance will be out. He also said he doesn't know if he will 'be with' Becky again – he does not want to keep doing what they have done. AND he said, "I'm happy."

Wednesday December 14, 2016

I posted in a Facebook group, an update about how Bryan is doing. The first response from a woman was, "That's great news but remember their moods can change daily."

It set a tone of disappointment and discouragement. I am already on edge, and it didn't help.

I went to a training today for trauma work. The instructor embarrassed me when I was making an observation about addiction and trauma. I was confused, embarrassed, and pissed by how he treated me in the training and then did not even further explain himself to me.

NOTHING

Thursday December 15, 2016

I did yoga and a mindfulness meditation and some core strength work.

I asked him –

"What do you know now about yourself that you didn't know three weeks ago?"

He said, "I deserve to be happy and have a good life…"

Bryan called – he had an infected tooth; he went to the Dr. and got an antibiotic.

The training continued today, and I found the courage to speak up to the facilitator about the previous day. It went pretty well. I met a counselor who works in Augusta, and we were partners for a couple of the practice exercises during the training.

He sounds good; he is still doing his treatment – he said he may break up with Becky – he still feels conflicted. He is going out with his dad for a couple hours Saturday: Family Day is Saturday.

Friday December 16, 2016

I had appointments in Augusta. I called the counselor at the treatment center to check in that I am still going to Florida.

I scheduled to meet with her briefly at 3:00 and then with the family therapist at 10:00 on Tuesday.

I had three new clients this week, which is exciting, and they seem to be good for me to work with.

I got paid today and a bunch of insurance money came in.

NOTHING

Saturday December 17, 2016

I had a counselor appointment at 8:00 a.m. and then did some note writing for work.

I talked to Bryan for a short while
– He broke up with Becky!!
He saw her at a meeting.

He said, "'So, are you going to be able to come down at all?'"

Me: "No, cause I didn't know what the weather was going to be like, or if you would still be there."

(I found out later that he knew I was coming, but he was trying to see if I would tell.)

Sunday December 18, 2016

I woke up at 4:00 a.m. and got ready for the fair. I showered and applied for my trauma certification. We left for the fair at about 8:30 and were there until 5:00.

We finished packing.

NOTHING

Monday December 19, 2016

I got up at 3 a.m. I arrived at the airport in Florida at about 1:15 p.m. It took me almost two hours to travel 40 miles from the airport.

I surprised him – he gave me a huge hug and cried.
He thought I was coming Tuesday and not today.

I got to see Bryan for about an hour and then I had to leave.

We went to an AA meeting – I met him there and it was a huge meeting! He introduced me to a lot of people he knows.

Tuesday December 20, 2016

I stopped at DD and got stuff for Bryan and his house mates.

We met with his counselor and the family counselor.

It was a very powerful and emotional session – held hands and looked at each other and shared strength and positive words and feelings about each other with each other.

I picked up lunch for us both. Zaxby's – buffalo chicken ranch sandwich, plain, fries, and birthday cake milkshake. We ate – I met the owner of the facility – then left about 1:30 to fly home.

Wednesday December 21, 2016

I had six clients today that started at 8:30 and ended at 7:30 at night.

I was tired but felt good.

NOTHING

Thursday December 22, 2016

I did a little work in the morning.

We had a quick call – all is good.

I had an interview for a fee for service job at an **IOP** to work as a mental health counselor for the clients there.

I had three appointments in the afternoon.

I was tired, really feeling good and happy, a little more relaxed regarding Bryan and change.

Friday December 23, 2016

I was home – Heather and Jeff came for dinner.

Stephen and I walked the golf course. Baked cookies.

We went to see their house – they move in two days!

NOTHING

Saturday December 24, 2016

Stephen and I went snow shoeing for about an hour.

We came home, showered, and then went to Farmington. We did a little shopping, went to the movies. A nice day.

NOTHING

Sunday December 25, 2016

I felt sick, a cold starting.

I ate breakfast and wrote my notes for work.

> Bryan called and said he is hoping to start planning to go to HWH – he is frustrated with some things going on there. Went and cleaned at Heather and Jeff's house.

Sat on the couch and watched TV and rested.

> He said he may try to call tomorrow with his counselor.

Heather came over for dinner.

My brain started – getting worried about Bryan regressing and 'giving up' again. Guess the Pink Cloud is done?

Monday December 26, 2016

I did some work in the morning.

Went to lunch in Portsmouth and met family there. We did Christmas with the kids and my mother and sister.

I thought Bryan was going to call with his counselor. Disappointed.

I have a bad feeling (or thought) that he is slipping – trying to keep the anxiety at bay.

I had a cold, felt kind of sick.

NOTHING

Tuesday December 27, 2016

Heather and Jeff – big truck moving day!!!

We went to dinner to celebrate.

I forced myself to stay awake – he said he would call…I was so tired.

9:37 p.m. I turned my phone off.

Maybe something happened. He didn't want to tell me. Is he talking to Becky again?

NOTHING

Wednesday December 28, 2016

I had four appointments today – all showed. Good!!

I wondered if I would hear anything today.

3:50 p.m.

I talked to the counselor – she said he is doing well – he shared his life story – had some good insights about his life.

He is still trying to keep his boundaries – not call every day. I felt sad, and happy at the same time.

Thursday December 29, 2016

I had appointments scheduled, but a big snowstorm was coming, and so everyone canceled.

I rested, hung out with Stephen, and worked on gathering information for the parent support group.

5:09 p.m.

"Hi Mom! Sorry I didn't call the other day – I wanted to give you a chance to practice some patience" …laughter…

He will be working on applying for jobs
– asked if I could help with rent for HWH.

I felt better having talked to the counselor – still adjusting to the idea of Bryan taking care of himself more.

Friday December 30, 2016

I was awake about 4:30 a.m. there was a big snow snowstorm overnight, about 16 inches.

Stephen started snow blowing at 6:00 - Heather and Jeff came over about 6:45; Jeff left for work about 7:00.

I went over with Heather and helped her shovel out the rest of her driveway.

I had one client in the middle of the day.

We watched a movie. I was still struggling with anxiety about Bryan.

NOTHING

Saturday December 31, 2016

We went snow shoeing.

I hung out at the house and was in bed early.

6:57 p.m.

"Hi Mom. I got my date to go to HWH. January 12. Things are going good. We are getting ready to watch a game so I'm looking forward to it. Could you maybe send some money so we can get a pizza? I'm gonna call dad too…"

January 2017

Sunday January 1, 2017

We had more snow overnight – three inches.

I went snow shoeing by myself.

Feeling really anxious about Bryan:

Is he ready for all the change? Does he have the skills he needs? What if he slips and then just says F-it?

NOTHING

Monday January 2, 2017

I had coffee with a friend in the morning and then went hiking with Stephen.

Grocery shopping.

We saw the movie, *Collateral Beauty* – I loved it…though it made me cry a bit.

Rested.

I talked to Bill. Becky got kicked out of the program she was at today – Bryan doesn't know yet. He didn't hear from Bryan yesterday either. He is planning to go to family weekend again.

NOTHING

Tuesday January 3, 2017

I had an appointment in the morning.

I walked in the woods with Stephen.

I met for coffee with another mom with a child with an addiction – we talked for two hours - we may work on a bill together to be able to involuntarily commit an addict – exciting stuff.

I talked with another friend – she happened to meet a good friend of ours – she is going to a group meditation; very happy - good energy all around.

Heather and Jeff closed on their house!

8:54 p.m.

"Hi Mom – I'm ready to move on to the next step. Next week – HWH. I haven't read any of your book – I've been reading the Big Book…I'll talk to you Friday. I heard Becky got kicked out; I'm so done with all of that."

Wednesday January 4, 2017

Full day – five clients, all showed up!

Feeling happy, content with a slight tinge of fear, anxiety… what if? Will it last?

NOTHING

Thursday January 5, 2017

Went for a nice walk in the woods with Stephen, using our yak traks.

It was a nice walk, but I felt out of sorts – maybe the anxiety caught up.

I went to a healing meditation with Stephen at a friend's shop… Good.

8:52 p.m.

"Hi Mom – kinda having a hard time – girl got kicked out because she gave me her iPod touch and I went on FB. I'm mad at Becky and I'm just having a bad day. I'm gonna just go to bed and I'll talk to you Saturday."

This really didn't help my anxiety. I slept, and I worked on keeping my focus on me and my life and my recovery.

Friday January 6, 2017

Morning meditation.

Went for a short walk in the woods.

Had three appointments that went well.

I got a call; I got a part time mental health job working with clients who are in IOP, yay!

I talked to Bryan's counselor – we talked about the issue, and she reassured me that he is still doing well and that they will work with him. I told her about some things I am sending for him and that we are planning a trip in March.

NOTHING

Saturday January 7, 2017

I wrote my notes from the week – then Stephen and I took a drive south and ended up in Wiscasset – had a great lunch. Did grocery shopping for the week – I got photos developed, bought frames – and got some new boots.

4:40 p.m.

"Hi Mom, I'm with Dad – we just went to Longhorn and I ate too fast. I have a pass – so I'll call you tonight."

8:41 p.m.

"Hi Mom! I'm doing good. I'm ready to go to HWH – had a good day with Dad; we talked about some different stuff. I'm tired of all the drama with the girls – I told him we are planning a trip in March to see him."

Sunday January 8, 2017

I woke up at 4 a.m.

I went for coffee with Stephen, Heather, a neighbor, and her daughter.

Then I crashed for the rest of the day – tired.

I posted on my mom sites – a photo of Bryan, and I wrote about how many days clean – 39 days – and that is the same number of times he has been to rehab.

I got a lot of positive support and feedback.

I started booking a trip to Florida for March.

NOTHING

Monday January 9, 2017

It was cold outside.

I did some shopping – had dinner and pizza with Heather and Jeff.

I put some money on Bryan's account to be used for cigarettes and groceries.

The anxiety is building as it gets closer to HWH day.

NOTHING

Tuesday January 10, 2017

I talked to the housing guy – he told me the process for paying for HWH – I told him and Bryan that I would cover two weeks.

I realized this is a new experience for us all.

My anxiety goes to what-ifs:

- He relapses
- He dies
- He gets discouraged and goes back out

THEN! The billing people called – insurance refreshes, $800 deductible, $2,300 out of pocket. "Is there anyone who can pay this?" The anxiety goes through the roof...should I pay? Make him pay? If it doesn't get paid, will he be homeless?

I didn't even think we had a deductible, and now I'm confused!!

I feel sick.

4:33 p.m.

"Hi Mom! I have 1 more day inpatient then I graduate – I'm proud of this accomplishment. I'm excited – gonna go to meetings, work steps with my sponsor. I just have to keep doing the right things."

Wednesday January 11, 2017

I woke up feeling anxious. I did a meditation, yoga, and a strength work out.

I did some work for work, paid for a week of Bryan's housing, talked to a few people. I called insurance to check benefits.

I felt better:

Distraction

Focus on me – what I can change

Trusting him and HP

Shopping – bought photo frames

I mailed out two packages to people: Mom/Bryan

Had appointments that went well.

NOTHING

Thursday January 12, 2017

I had some appointments in the afternoon.

2:35 p.m.

I got a phone call...he got out of PHP.

"Hi Mom! I feel good, I'm happy."

I vacillated between being so happy and scared to death.

I confirmed this week that I will be starting a part- time job seeing clients at the IOP; I will be their mental health counselor, and they want me to start a family program for them...I already developed a curriculum!

8:24 p.m.

"Hey, I'm at a meeting. It starts at 8:30 – just wanted to check in. Love you."

Friday January 13, 2017

I had an awesome 8:30 appointment at the house – then five appointments in Augusta.

Bryan went shopping with his dad – posted on Facebook.

It was a good day – I picked up Chinese food for me and Stephen.

I booked a trip for me and Stephen to go to Florida.

11:37 p.m.

"Awesome I cannot wait I love you – call you in the morning."

I woke up in the middle of the night – I missed a call from Heather – Bryan had texted and message from a friend.

I had a three-hour stretch of insomnia – worried about kids, thinking about work...ugggh.

Saturday January 14, 2017

Stephen and I walked the golf course.

11:32 a.m.

"Going to play basketball have a good afternoon Love you!"

Then I went to Hallowell with Heather and to lunch and did some shopping.

An enjoyable day, then met a friend for a drink.

3:31 p.m.

"God, it feels good to be able to play basketball for 3 hours again."

Me: :)

Stephen held a Reiki share.

Facebook posts kind of crazy – it seems like he was all over the place.

Sunday January 15, 2017

Yoga

Circuit training

Walked the dogs

Bryan called at 7:58 a.m.

He was getting ready to go to work.
He was then going to meet up with his sponsor.

Did some work for my job.

Holding a sign for a store – seven hours, $50.

I spent more time with Heather – grocery shopping, went for coffee.

Stephen went to Massachusetts to visit the kids.

I was conscious all day of not calling/texting

Resisting the urge to know what's going on.

Monday January 16, 2017

He called at night – my phone never rang...

I did some notes in the morning.

I had a dentist appointment.

8:02 a.m. text:

"You working today?"

"No not today, I'm looking 4 jobs."

Me: "ok – how'd you sleep?"

"Great actually. Yesterday was long but good though."

Me: "Woot! I'm glad. Good luck on job search. Ttyl my son."

"Thank you. Love you."

11:35 a.m.

"Great day so far mother."

"What made your day great?"

"Beautiful day with good people. Sobriety is great. Great friends."

I had lunch with Heather and Jeff - rested in the afternoon.

Naranon – seven people came, including us!

A lot of newbies – angry, sad, struggling. Makes me feel a little guilty…things are going well for us.

Tuesday January 17, 2017

Did some work.

8:49 a.m. – phone call

"Good morning. I just wanted to check in. I'm going to hold the sign today."

Walked the dogs.

Had one appointment – good one!

HR at my new part time job at 1:00.

> 12:46 p.m.

> "I got 2 jobs!! 1 of them is right across the street from the HWH the other is 3 miles away!"

Came home, did some more work – hung out with Stephen.

> 7:47 p.m.

> "I'm thinking of going to a new HWH, IOP – it would only be 3 days a week so I can work more. I'm gonna pray about it and talk to my support network. Will you pray, too?"

Excitement for Bryan – hopeful and right next to it – anxiety and preparedness that it won't last.

I prayed – had a sinking déjà vu feeling. Like he's going to keep running.

> 9:25 p.m. – Facebook post:

> "In life, it's hard to see who I could trust"

Wednesday January 18, 2017

I woke up with some clarity of what I want to say. I texted it because I envisioned an argument/debate. In the past he would ask for advice and then argue with it. I really didn't want to do that. I sent the text – anxious, afraid of a return to the arguing – and a small hope that this time will be different.

> He decided to stay where he is – he had talked to some people.

"Stay in the day, Karen," I said to myself.

Relief – such a roller-coaster of fear and faith.

Thursday January 19, 2017

yoga

circuit training

walked dogs

work

10:32 p.m. – text

"One of my close friends relapsed last night. I was supposed to go with him yesterday. I didn't know he was gonna get high. I will not throw this away. I love you."

Felt relief; he said he is staying.

Trust is growing, slowly

Just gotta keep doing what I'm doing.

Meditation circle.

Friday January 20, 2017

"More people kicked out for drinking or using."

I walked the dogs, then I went for a run with Stephen.

7:58 a.m.

"grateful that I have a car so I can get myself out of these situations."

I did some work for a couple of hours.

Smaller shifts in trust/faith/fear…

Will he stay clean? How would I know? Don't want to get too comfortable…uggghh.

7:53 p.m. – text

"I'm so glad you have decided that you are worth it… there is truly no limit to how amazing your life can be! ! Sending you hugs and prayers… always!"

9:16 p.m.

"I love you mother. Thank you."

Saturday January 21, 2017

Went to woman's march with Heather and Stephen. Bryan video called.

I couldn't hear but was able to blow him kisses.

5:22 p.m.

He called, had gotten out of work. He was going to go to a meeting then go out with some friends.

Spent the day with Heather/Stephen.

Trying to appreciate "one day at a time."

Sunday January 22, 2017

Had lunch with Heather and Jeff.

Text:

"Had a great day with dad and a friend and had 53 days and watched horrible football games and got my shoulder cut open."

Hung out with Stephen.

At night he posted that a tornado flipped his car, and he was hiding in a closet. I didn't find this out until the next morning.

Monday January 23, 2017

7:12 a.m.

"Did your car really get flipped?"

8:45 a.m.

"No! I was joking!"

"Love you.... Lol"

Grrrr...

Did some work.

Went for a walk – in the woods with Stephen.

2:08 p.m.

"Just went to a meeting"

I went to a meeting, five people total, yay!!

He called about 8 p.m. – "kid from PHP died."

8:35 p.m. – text

"I feel for his family. It hurts seeing people die.
It's crazy to think that a week after I saw him, he was dead."

"I know, I read every single day, multiple times a day, moms telling
how they 'got the call' – I pray for them and for you and all the
sick and suffering."

"I know it's not fair, It's so prevalent in my life.
It sickens me. Scares me."

He said he went to two meetings and PHP to try to make sense
of it all – also talked to his sponsor.

Tuesday January 24, 2017

Did work on our LLC – and addiction fundraiser.

I created a Naranon flyer and sent in notices for the meeting.

He hung out with a friend – they went to the water
and just sat there.

I had an appointment in the afternoon – Good appointment...
mental health and addiction.

Snow, sleet, rain all day.

5:15 p.m. – I texted him

No answer by 7:05, phone went right to voicemail.

Called Bill – he expressed concern about Bryan's commitment.

7:51 p.m. – text

"I'm fine – I was at a meeting – I'll call you later"

Imagination went right to fear:

Will he stay clean?

Will he OD?

Will he die?

8:21 p.m.

"I had a good day – I learned some lessons so even
though it was stressful I am taking something away."

Wednesday January 25, 2017

Shoveled in the morning with Stephen.

56 days clean.

Bryan called on his way to work.

I'm working for the next five days.
It will be a lot but it's good.

I told him that my trust in him is growing every day. My fears spike
at times, and it's hard. I asked if there was something that would
be helpful for me to do more, or less. He said, "Don't call Dad."

His Dad really puts pressure on him.

Talked about budgeting money and balancing time.

"I need to not expect too much from others
early in recovery, even for me."

He's not the old Bryan – he's a new Bryan.

Called at 8:01 p.m.

Becky wanted to do ninth step. Talked about stuff – family is back in her life – It was one of the best decisions I could have made – getting healthy boundaries could have saved our lives. Good to see she's alive.

"Mom, I think you need to use your supports and not call dad…"

Thursday January 26, 2017

Got stuck in driveway – ice!!

Went to the new job.

Long day – only saw one client but was glad for that.

"My tire popped so I had to get it fixed and did and then got my hair cut then went to work…:)"

I have to learn a new computer system.

Didn't talk to Bryan much – paid rent

Less and less worry every day – feels unsettling still – but happy to feel lighter and less anxious.

Noah's Birthday.

Friday January 27, 2017

Meditation

Yoga

Circuit training

He asked for $30 to go out go-carting with friends. He will re-pay me for that and this past week's rent.

Work – saw three clients.

He worked from 8-5 p.m., then went to IOP.

I had to decide whether to send money:

Will he really pay it back? Will he use it for what he said?

Saturday January 28, 2017

8:42 a.m.

"Another girl died yesterday…I'm still here though."

"I love you so much, I know God has a plan for us all…trying to trust the process…"

"Worked 10 – 3, then met with sponsor."

Went to Massachusetts – for eye appointment; visit with friends and the kids.

He went out last night – they didn't go go-carting; they ended up going to Olive Garden. "It was terrible, it was so expensive. I had a steak, and it was like $20. I won't ever eat there again."

I talked to him later in the evening; he said he was really tired.

He is living life, having everyday experiences that he should have; will it last?

60 DAYS!!!!!

Sunday January 29, 2017

Got up and left kind of early from Massachusetts.

"60 days today! I know I have been slipping a little with my meetings lately. I am going to a meeting now, then I am speaking to the PHP – they ask someone who has been through it, to come back and speak. Then I'm meeting with my sponsor."

He Face-timed us while we were in the car.

I continue to be grateful for every day he is clean and taking steps into his life. I feel like I don't know how to talk to him or what to talk about now.

> Dad came to my friend's house last night – I got an extension on my curfew, and my phone died, so dad couldn't reach me. He needs to focus on himself...

Monday January 30, 2017

Walked dogs.

I did some work in the office.

A client came in with an emergency.

Secured a new client – a couple where addiction is an issue.

3:45 p.m.

"Hey son. I hope you had a good day. Getting ready to go to dinner and then a meeting. Send me a text about your day...love you so much!"

Dinner with Stephen and Jeff – quick dinner.

> "I will, I love you. Okay good stuff. I'm tired mother. I will be able to rest tomorrow."

Naranon speaker – Good meeting.

> 10:40 p.m. – Facebook post:

> "I seen way too many RIP statuses today."

Very little obsession – low anxiety.

Tuesday January 31, 2017

I texted at 7:15 a.m.

Did some yoga, had a no-show from a potential first appointment.

Walked the dogs after my 2:30 appointment no-showed.

3:30 appointment came.

5:00 went to a client's house for appointment.

Feeling irritated, no calls/texts then...

I called him at 7:00 – he sounded good – said he went to two meetings today.

9:34 p.m. – text

"I just talked to Doug video chat – he's doing horrible. :("

11:11 p.m. – Facebook post:

"It kills me seeing the one I love most struggle the most."

12:30 a.m. – text

"Oh no! I'm sorry!"

"I love you so much"

"It's ok. Pray for him. That's all we can do."

"I love you."

February 2017

Wednesday February 1, 2017

5:45 a.m. – text

"I love you so much."

I did yoga, got ready for work.

Had an appointment in the morning – did some work on the office.

Lunch with Jeff and Stephen- he was getting ready for work.

11:15 a.m.

"call me tonight at 8"

Afternoon appointments, good day! I was busy – felt good about all.

4:41 p.m. – Facebook message:

"I am sad about Doug I'm feeling worried,
and I love you and miss you."

I called at 8…no answer.

Saw him on Facebook – texted at 8:08:

"I know you're probably just finishing group…"

8:50 tried to video chat –

Nothing

Texted: "You told me to call – I tried. Going to sleep – up about 5 – I don't like being ignored."

8:54 p.m. – Facebook message:

"Sorry Mom. I have a lot going on right now. I love you…. sorry"

"I know, I can tell, and it worries me."

"Please just take care of yourself and keep your supports close."
– (seen at 11:59)

Thursday February 2, 2017

I woke up at 3 a.m. to go to the bathroom – saw this text from Bill that was sent at 11:39:

"Bryan used tonight; he is at my house. I can't get him help until tomorrow. He can't go back to HWH."

So, I got up and made coffee – I tried to go back to sleep, but my mind said, "No!"

I went to work for 10:00 and talked to Bryan – he was talking about leaving Florida; has to get out – but was gonna wait until Monday –

"I want to watch the super bowl," he said.

By the afternoon, communication stopped. By evening, no one had heard from him since 3:00 – no Facebook activity, phone not trackable.

I talked to a HWH manager who was expecting him in the evening.

Stephen and I went to meditation group – I cried a lot but was able to relax a bit.

I was afraid he would die; I envisioned the funeral – do people take pictures of their loved ones?

I talked to Bill about 9:00 – we are both sad and scared.

Bill texted me at 10:45, "Bryan called me from Longwood hospital in Ft. Peirce, he's ok, he is safe tonight and will call in the morning." (I saw this text at 12:00.)

NOTHING

Friday February 3, 2017

2:01 a.m. – Facebook message:

> "I love you I'm ok."

> He had been discharged from the hospital at 10:00 p.m. the night before.

(I saw his message at 4:53 a.m. and responded.)

"I love you."

I felt relief that he was in the hospital. I called the hospital at 6:30 a.m. and they said he was discharged at about 10 p.m.

I looked up plane tickets to get him out of Florida.

I had to work – I had six appointments – I didn't know where he was all day.

By 1:00 p.m. no one had heard anything – no activity on FB. All I could think was that he was dead somewhere, alone. Was it an "OD? Was it guns?

> 2:00 p.m.

> Bill found Bryan -– he was with him now.

6:27 p.m.

He called me; said he was going to get food. He said he was staying in a hotel with his ex-girlfriend and some others.

Missed calls:

10:34 p.m. – Unknown number - two

10:37 p.m. – Another number – two

10:44 p.m. – text from Bill

"Call me!!!!" (I was sleeping)

10:48 p.m. – Bill called – Twice

I woke up at 2:00 a.m. – looked at my phone – saw five missed calls; my heart raced – I jumped out of bed – called Bill – Bryan was found naked, unresponsive – his heart had stopped. I sat in the living room, staring at the floor…numb.

Saturday February 4, 2017

I was able to fall back to sleep until 6:30 a.m.

I called the hospital – they were Marchman acting him – hold for 72 hours.

He overdosed two nights in a row.

I had plans to meet up with a co-worker for breakfast and spend some time with Heather.

I was exhausted, anxious, not fully understanding of what had happened and how – it was so fast.

I had breakfast, then went to acupuncture with Heather.

I talked to Bryan early afternoon – he was at the facility for assessment – they let him go before the 72 hours!!!! How could they do that?!

He was agitated and irritable.

He agreed to come north and get out of Florida.

His dad brought him to get a phone
– he sent me that number late at night.

I was anxious and on edge the rest of the day. I found a flight for early in the a.m. from Ft. Lauderdale to Boston; he was accepted to go to a program in New Hampshire.

He told me he knew he died – lost control of his bladder and bowels. He saw God and Noah, and they were all holding hands – then they let him go and he woke up…they had revived him with the paddles.

Sunday February 5, 2017

I kept my phone with me all night – looked at it all night.

At 3:15 a.m. – I got up and stayed up. I chatted with Bryan a bit and he said…

Family weekend is next weekend.

I wrote notes for work.

3:55 a.m.

"I'm getting on the plane don't worry. I'll see you in the north northeast."

"Ok…I was just thanking my moms for all their prayers for you… and I continue to pray for us all."

3:57 a.m.

"Thank you mom. I was seconds away from death now I'm coming back."

"I know…I hope you don't forget…it wasn't your time. I hope your life is long and you get to bless many people with your heart and spirit.

"I'm just scared for what's in front of me."

"What part scares you? That you don't know what it is?"

"Everything."

4:02 a.m.

"I am not sure it could be much worse than what is behind you. Other than death. Keep reaching out and tell people those things… it helps to tell people your truth and fears."

He got to the airport – didn't have money for baggage. We finally got it worked out – he made it on the plane.

He arrived in Boston around 10 a.m. – he got a ride from the treatment center in New Hampshire.

> Bryan called in the afternoon – he said he is struggling and really beating himself up. He is cold and really doesn't know why he came here. He said pride is what kept him from going back to the treatment center that he left – he was embarrassed. He said after he reached 60 days – he just stopped doing what he needed to.
> He is miserable.

I took a shower.

Heather and Jeff came over for lunch – we ate and watched *SNL* and had some good laughs.

I took a little nap and finished work for the week.

I am hoping we can go to see him tomorrow to bring him some warmer clothes.

I am afraid he will want to leave.

Monday February 6, 2017

7:30 a.m. – called treatment center. The person I spoke to said that the center is open from 7:30 - to 5:00.

And they said it wouldn't be a problem for me to bring clothes to him and see him.

The case manager was going to call me later.

I went shopping and missed a call from New Hampshire – called back and left a message.

While on the way to New Hampshire, Bryan called, and we had a conversation about him wanting to leave.

> Phone call: "I just want to spend time with you. I'm tired of visiting in these places. I don't want to be here. I just wanted to come and see you and spend time."

What do I do?

Take him?

Leave him?

Turn around and not go at all?

Stephen and I talked about it for an hour and a half – we kind of landed that we would take him – out of fear that he would leave.

We arrived and several of the staff spoke to us.

We weren't allowed to see him. They convinced us to leave him there…

I was so sad – it physically hurt me.

We left clothes for him.

I cried a lot of the way home. We stopped for dinner – then went to Naranon – STEP 2.

I missed a call at night from the family counselor from Florida… I couldn't sleep.

Tuesday February 7, 2017

I woke up feeling exhausted.

I was angry and sad. I took it out a little on Stephen.

He went to the counselor, and I had a client appointment.

It snowed… appointment canceled.

Did some paperwork, sent emails, scheduled other appointments.

I talked to the case manager and the family counselor who is coming for family day.

Bryan was not phased much by us leaving, they said.

He still wants to leave treatment and return to Florida.

I feel like he was manipulating me – I feel overwhelmed by the fears that he may die, and the other possibility, that he lingers in this way for decades.

I'm tired and will try to stay strong for Family Day.

NOTHING

Wednesday February 8, 2017

I slept through the night – forced myself to not look at the phone during the night.

I received an email in the a.m. from the case manager saying that Bryan and another kid (who just arrived the day before from Florida) were in the process of signing themselves out of treatment.

About an hour and a half later, she confirmed they left.

I was so mad and sad and confused and hurt.

Where will he go?

It's so cold out – did he have clothes?

What is he thinking?

I canceled the hotel – no family weekend for us.

When will I ever get to hug him now?! He had almost died, and I just wanted to touch him…I was so close. How could I live with myself if he died now? I thought I was doing the responsible and healthy thing.

Should I have taken him?

How will we all get through this?

4:17 p.m. – text

"I'm at the airport."

"I can't talk about it. I will talk to you when you are in recovery… I don't want to hear excuses, how you have nothing, and no one understands…I won't pay for anything else. I love you; I know you know that.

I continue to pray for you, but I cannot see an outcome I like right now. I do look forward to seeing you do well, but you have to do it. I don't want to hear the play by play; it hurts too much."

"Treatment isn't recovery."

"Just text every now and then so I know you're alive. It's the least you can do…please."

5:17 p.m.

"Ok"

7:40 p.m.

"All I wanted was to spend time with you. I still do. You win."

If he dies, will I blame myself and regret that decision? Most likely, I will…

Thursday February 9, 2017

Text: "???"

BLIZZARD

I thought he was flying out at six; he said the flight was changed to 3 p.m. Most flights were canceled due to blizzard – Day 2 at Logan airport.

5:26 a.m.

"My friend is in a coma brain dead right now"

"Who?! I'm so sorry. Where are you now?"

"Tonya. I was just in PHP with her."

"I'm at Logan waiting for my flight."

"And there really isn't any 'winning'….and I am not in competition with you…"

"I'm so sad right now"

"I know. Me too."

"I don't want to put another rip status. I was actually close with
                                                                    her."

"Where will you go?"

                                                                "What?"

"Going to Florida? Where? Doing what?"

                                                            "Call me"

We talked a little...at least I heard his voice. We ended on a
better note.

                                    Texted a little, then nothing.

Stephen and I walked at the golf course.

I cried a little this morning – I was thanking Stephen for just being
here with me through all this.

Canceled all appointments for clients.

Did some paperwork.

Heather came over – we played with the dogs.

                                                        11:00 p.m.

                        They missed the connection – he is stuck in
                        Atlanta overnight. Good sleep for me.

Is it wrong to feel a little happy or smug that he got stuck at
the airport?

Is God or something intervening and keeping him from Florida?

Why?

I started to compile a list of his Facebook friends that I was going
to enlist as a virtual intervention. I did not get very far with that.
Feeling desperate.

Friday February 10, 2017

6:00 a.m.

I cried first thing in the morning – the questions started:

Should I have brought him here?

Should I file a Baker or Marchman Act?

Will he live or die?

Will I see him again?

Does he think I don't care?

I had two appointments at the office, two at the house.

Work is a good distraction.

I wonder if there will come a time when I don't have to hold it together?

Will I fall apart?

4:43 p.m. – text message

"Here."

4:49 p.m. – text message:

"ok, take good care... I love you."

I feel a little more relaxed – though I have no idea about his plans – or treatment level – maybe this time?

Saturday February 11, 2017

More snow

Did some shopping.

Rested – really tired.

It occurred to me that he only has three months left of good in-surance – if he lives that long – maybe it will be better with none?

He will have to be serious and motivated.

Planning on creating a curriculum for parents AND want to sign up to do a presentation for my colleagues about addiction and the family.

I watched a movie with Stephen.

Feeling slightly more settled into my life.

Talked to my old Alanon sponsor...it could be helpful to return to some step work.

Did some reading in ACOA book – I am pretty codependent...sigh.

NOTHING

Sunday February 12, 2017

I did a meditation in the morning.

Finished some work for my job.

Shoveling.

Snowshoe walk at the golf course.

Feel detached – It's a feeling – I can't describe how I did it, couldn't tell anyone else how to detach...

Watched a movie.

Worked on presentation for work.

9:32 p.m. – text from Bill:

"Bryan left detox, chasing after Becky. I am turning my phone off until tomorrow."

NOTHING

Monday February 13, 2017

BLIZZARD

On Facebook – approximately 3 a.m.:

> "F-in disgusted. Hurt beyond belief. Who the
> f. have you become and what the f. did
> you do to my best friend???"

> (About Becky?)

Had a 7:30 a.m. video session with counselor. Examining my thoughts and feelings about what I do and why.

Some old guilt about things I have done and not done... unresolved issues form my relationship with my mother.

We stayed in all day – I resisted the urge to contact him – until later in the day.

Text:

"Praying...moms are praying."

> "I know"

7:10 p.m.

"I do pray you rest well and know I love you so much and believe in you!! Gampy's birthday today... I sent a photo."

> "I love you Mom."

Tuesday February 14, 2017

Blizzard clean-up.

Shoveled and worked outside most of the morning.

Went to lunch with Stephen.

Continued to feel anxious to know what direction Bryan will go. Not knowing is the hardest.

1:41 p.m.

Voicemail from Bryan:

"Hi Mom. I just wanted to let you know that I'm going somewhere today and I'm so sorry for putting you through all of this. I love you so much, Mom."

When I/we ask for support, people aren't always helpful. So, we talked through how to manage the feedback.

11:40 p.m.

"They're picking me up at 8, well in the morning."

So happy to hear there may be some movement into some treatment and hopefully back on track.

Wednesday February 15, 2017

8:11 a.m.

"Are you on your way?" Called and texted several times.

NOTHING.... phone on, goes to voicemail.

Crying, afraid he's dead somewhere. I don't know where he is or who he is with.

What if he just wanted to use one more time before detox, and then died?

Part of me wanted his pain and suffering to end – live in recovery or die.

Who would that be easier for, me or him?

12:28 p.m.

"I didn't hear from you, and I thought bad things..."

12:51 p.m.

"I'm sorry mom. I was sleeping. I love you. I'll call you in a bit.

1:23 p.m.

"I don't wanna worry you guys anymore."

1:32 p.m.

"I love you so much. I hope to see you next month."

"You will mother."

I had four client appointments, made cookies and banana bread… some relief.

7:40 p.m.

I called him.

(Screaming on the phone)

"Mom, we went in, and someone freaked out and they kicked us out – we called the police, I'll call you back."

8:45 p.m.

I called back; he was going to be picked up.

10:23 p.m.

"I'm with them."

11:37 p.m.

"Ok…stay safe please. I love you so much…"

11:38 p.m.

"I will mother. I will. I'm sorry for all this."

Thursday February 16, 2017

3:16 a.m.

"I'm here – I love you."

I left the house at 9:00, had to go to the IOP.

I was supposed to have five appointments, ended up with one. I got home at 5:15 p.m. – uggghh!

Received a call from the detox – she said Bryan was resting and talking about going to treatment.

Today I feel some relief that he is safe, but… he could walk out any time. He has been to at least 40 detoxes.

I don't want to be too excited. But – I won't look at my phone all night.

Friday February 17, 2017

I had some work – four appointments – preparing the office. Our Open House of our Wellness Center.

My worry level is lower today.

I do have some guilt – a little happy that I can just live my life – Alanon would say, "You can do that anyway…find happiness whether they are drinking or using or not." Though it is true, it is a challenging practice at times.

I have tried to live my life – but when he is out running around, I have difficulty not waiting for "the call" that could come at any time.

If my son had cancer – would someone, anyone, tell me to put him out of my mind?

You have to let him go?

I don't think so….

NOTHING

Saturday February 18, 2017

I got up, did my notes for work.

I prepared the office for the Open House for the Wellness Center.

I had several friends come between 12-4 and had a really nice visit with them.

"Hey Mom – I'm doing ok – I'm really mad that all
my clothes were stolen – my good sneakers, 2 pairs,
and they said, 'Well, you shouldn't have walked out.'"

"Can you send me a book? I'm looking for a
book about the Law of Attraction"

Bryan called in the middle – I had just "picked up a card" from
my science cards – Freedom.

On one hand I was glad to hear his voice (even though it was really
clear that he was quite heavily medicated, which only reminds me
of him being high); on the other hand, I felt discouraged that all
he seemed to care about was his clothes…ummm aren't you at all
grateful for your life?! It doesn't seem like it…

Sunday February 19, 2017

After having a great event yesterday, I did a nice meditation this
morning. I realized – despite his obsession about clothes, sounding
a bit hopeless, he did ask for a great book that could help – that
gave me hope – I will order it today.

I felt a little more hopeful that I found something to hold onto
that was positive.

NOTHING

Monday February 20, 2017

I did some work in the office to prepare the office for the week.

President's Day today – so couldn't do some work.

Stephen and I went for a drive down near Rockport to get a new
wood stove that was on sale. Had lunch.

Came back home, did some scheduling for the week.

Went to Naranon meeting – Stephen and I were the only ones
there – uggghh… texted Bill – they found Bryan's sneakers. He
said they had cut down his meds, and he sounded better.

Feeling a little more hopeful.

NOTHING

Tuesday February 21, 2017

I woke up at midnight and looked at the phone – Bryan had been on FB just shortly before – fell back to sleep fearful that he left detox – that he would die and that I would have to plan a funeral. Uggghhh…happy Tuesday.

I had four appointments during the day – went over to see Heather – she has determined they have to put their cat to sleep – he's too sick – she is devastated.

She came over for dinner – still sad – scheduled for the vet to come to her house tomorrow. Cat is in so much pain, she was crying, "He is right there, and I can't even pick him up…" I told her that's how I felt about Bryan – he's there, alive, but I can't be with him – and in New Hampshire I had to leave without seeing him.

10:08 p.m.

Text from Bill – "Bryan is still at the detox, Becky left;
he didn't, and she might have signed on his FB."

Wednesday February 22, 2017

I keep thinking that he gets out of detox soon - will he continue staying clean? Will there be another loss in our family?

I love my work and my job and really want to work harder on my marriage – I'm afraid that will slip away with my distraction and sadness about Bryan.

I went for a walk with Stephen at the golf course.

I had four appointments. Bryan called during one of them and left a voicemail.

I called back and the counselor answered.

Heather said, "I look at the healthy cats and get angry." I think, *I can relate to that...*that's what I think about others and their children.

Heather and Jeff decided to put their cat to sleep.

Bryan called during my evening appointment. I put $10 on his account. He called later:

> "You're hard to get ahold of. I don't think I'm going to PHP – I have to get a ride to PSL."

Thursday February 23, 2017

As Saturday gets closer, release from detox, I get more anxious.

I went to the IOP, part-time job, and three out of five clients showed up.

One of the supervisors asked about Bryan, that made me feel good...so few ask and then also listen to the answer.

Bryan said he would call – no call.

What does that mean?

Did he use the card for other calls?

Did he not want to talk to me again?

NOTHING

Friday February 24, 2017

I had six client appointments scheduled.

> 9:30 a.m.
>
> I called and talked to Bryan and counselor.
> He is adamant – he does not want to go to PHP,
> he said he will figure it out.
>
> 7:00 p.m.
>
> He was home at his dad's – they had plans
> to go to two games on the weekend.

I was somewhat worried about where he is going. I continue to say in my head, "It's all up to him…"

Saturday February 25, 2017

I got up – had breakfast with Stephen – after he took care of Heather and Jeff's animals – then we did yoga.

He went back over to their house and did some work there. I did work in the office.

9:18 a.m. – text

"I love you so much…I am still here, always, fighting for you… with you…"

"I know that I'm grateful for that."

"I went to a meeting tonight. It's hard to be back around people. No one said anything – I just felt a little bad."

Dinner and a movie with Stephen.

Sunday February 26, 2017

Breakfast and caught up on some shows.

Notes for work.

TEXTS AND FACEBOOK.

We were talking about how he was – he had reached out to some people, but no one had gotten back to him… I felt sad for him and frustrated.

Walked the dogs.

I talked to Bill – he struggles a lot with control and detachment.

Did filing in the office.

Some couples work with Stephen.

Unknown about what Bryan will do – I am working hard at staying strong and healthy in my thinking.

Monday February 27, 2017

I had a client in the morning.

TEXTS THROUGHOUT THE DAY ABOUT WHERE HE IS GOING – WHAT HE IS DOING.

Went to the Naranon meeting - no one else showed up.

Probably going to cancel it – I need support and there is no one here!!!

10:28 p.m.

"I feel like I'm being pressured into going into treatment. I'm going got get grandpa off dad's back and so you and dad can sleep. Looks like I'll be in treatment when you come see me again. :("

Tuesday February 28, 2017

Facebook and texts - from 12:59 a.m. until 2:18 a.m.

1:06 a.m.

"I want to give up, but I can't. I love you so much, Mom. You are amazing; you're my best friend I wouldn't be half the man I am today if I didn't have you."

I had several appointments during the day when he finally got picked up, it was around dinner time.

He has only been out of detox (had been there ten days) for four days – and going back!!

"I'm sorry for the pain and worry…I feel the pain and the powerless – we will keep fighting together, Mom – we will have a great story and we're going to touch many lives." (This has some to do with the pain and powerlessness he feels about Becky.)

I didn't think he had used, but apparently, he did…

Will he be able to stay clean?

I know it's possible because others do it...

He left a message at 9:20 p.m. (I was already asleep)
saying he was there and will call when he can.

March 2017

Wednesday March 1, 2017

I realized I don't even know the name of the facility…uggghhh…

9:16 a.m.

Call – missed it – no message.

NOTHING

I did a meditation, yoga, and walked.

I had several appointments during the day.

2:49 p.m.

I talked to the owner of the detox.

Thursday March 2, 2017

I had a counselor appointment; I told the counselor I didn't want to talk about Bryan…he was pleased with my statement.

12:44 p.m.

Bryan called while I was at work. He said he will call later because I was at work.

I worked at the IOP from 11 to 4. All four clients showed up. I do love my job…

Friday March 3, 2017

Stephen went to Massachusetts – to get tattoos with Beth for her birthday.

I had two appointments in Augusta.

And I called Mom – nice conversation.

24 years today since my brother died.

Late afternoon clients canceled, no- showed…grrrr…

Feeling settled with Bryan and where he is.

NOTHING

Saturday March 4, 2017

I went to breakfast at nine – but first I finished my work notes and some work.

It was a colleague breakfast – talking about some work issues.

I did a couple of errands, then went home.

I had a missed call and a message from Bryan while I was at breakfast.

> "Hi Mom – call me back at this number, with my case manager – I'm sorry if anyone called to say I was leaving. I'm still here."

It was freezing outside, so I stayed on the couch with the dogs.

I called back to the detox…

> He said, "Yeah, I was gonna leave with a kid; I honestly don't know why I didn't."

It makes me feel very unsettled when he doesn't even know why he does what he does. I was all happy and he could have been gone…

Sunday March 5, 2017

I went to Belfast with Heather for her last weekend before she starts working weekends. We did some shopping, breakfast, and then had a walk in the state park.

A real enjoyable day.

NOTHING

Monday March 6, 2017

I did some work around the house (organizing the office and house).

Grocery shopping with Heather and Jeff.

I had tea with a friend – did Angel cards with her – it was GOOD!

I made some phone calls for work and did some scheduling.

Six months until the bike ride!!!

> I talked to the case manager briefly – she said that Bryan is going to PHP, and he is doing great.

I feel relieved that he sounds like he is "back."

Tuesday March 7, 2017

I had a first appointment no show, but second one showed up and it was a good session – talked about ACOA (Adult Children of Alcoholics) - good stuff, good session!

Had some downtime with Stephen.

I had two later appointments, trauma work – good work!

I thought about Bryan – he is due to go to PHP tomorrow.

I thought:

He seems to do better the less we talk…is that true? Do I "trigger" him more than I know?

Would it be best for us to have more distance?

I would do that – keep more distance – if it meant he stays clean and is happy and healthy.

NOTHING

Wednesday March 8, 2017

I had appointments.

I had a couple cancellations, but also got a couple new clients. Had group supervision and it was good.

Today Bryan is supposed to go to PHP.

10 – 11 a.m. – no word.

12 - 1 p.m. – no word

2 - 3 p.m. - sinking feeling – just a 'knowing' that he is not going.

4:15 p.m. – Bill called.

He said Bryan went to the hospital – left and didn't want to go to PHP.

I talked to Bryan – texted briefly:

He said he has a broken vertebrae, wants to go to the hospital and have surgery… but has no plan – nowhere to go.

We go to Florida in eight days…don't know if he will be alive by then – if we will see him – don't know if I want to – if he's not even trying.

Thursday March 9, 2017

I looked at my phone through the night last night.

He was in pain, a lot, kept talking about surgery.

At 11:15, Bill texted saying Bryan was in a HWH in PSL – safe for the night.

He was stressed – in pain, confused – feels like we were forcing treatment on him.

I woke up thinking, *What if I tell him I'm giving up?*

Many texts on the phone

I can't do this anymore.

What if I said, "I think this is a great decision," like reverse psychology, would that work?

Manipulation…I just want him to see what I see…to change… to live.

> Bryan and I talked quite a bit – he has been feeling confused about treatment – doing things the way he wants – doesn't know who he can trust, including me and his dad.

I tried to go to work – cried a lot on the way – I couldn't go. I felt guilty, but couldn't stop crying.

I walked the dogs, had coffee with Heather, rested on the couch with Stephen.

I fell asleep about 8 p.m.

Friday March 10, 2017

I woke up about 2 a.m. and couldn't go back to sleep.

I got up about 3:45 a.m. - wrote my notes, did some EMDR research, took a shower.

I texted Bryan encouraging him to do EMDR for addictions and/ or trauma.

We talked some…

I went to work – saw a few clients – finished at 3 p.m.

He is at IOP – says he doesn't want to use.

We talked my whole ride home – about addiction – his side and my side.

"I know I need to let others help me – I don't have all the answers."

I have hope again – willingness.

Saturday March 11, 2017

We had a Reiki class – Stephen taught it – I was a participant – I was tired in the morning but felt better by the afternoon.

11:56 a.m.

He sent a screen shot of a text from his ex-girlfriend – she had overdosed and was in treatment – talking about how others were trying to help her – and she was asking him for help – he wrote to me:

"This is what I wake up to. Chaos. Pure chaos."

I said I'm sorry and will pray for her and him.

"Just a reminder of what I don't wanna go back to."

12:44 p.m.

"I don't wanna die."

12:46 p.m.

"I know. Right now, you are alive, and you are learning how to live."

12:59 p.m.

"I love you, Mom."

1:02 p.m.

"I love you beyond words."

Will it stick?

Will he live?

I want to believe…I feel guilty if I have doubts.

Sunday March 12, 2017

9:05 a.m. – text

"Call me when you get up, I have some news."

9:05 a.m.

"What is it?"

"good stuff – sorry…"

Stephen and I did a distance Reiki healing for Bryan in the a.m.

He called about a half an hour later – he said he thought something bad had happened – I knew that's what he thought…

We talked about the weekend and that maybe we could go and get tattoos on Saturday for my birthday.

I drove to Kittery to meet my sister for lunch and a visit.

We shopped, chatted, and had a pretty good visit.

We did a Full Moon meditation and energy share here at the house/Wellness Center. Two other people came; it was really nice.

Monday March 13, 2017

I had morning appointments.

I texted him.

"6:06 a.m. – good morning. I have appts. at 9 and 10:30 this morning. Love you!"

8:28 a.m.

"So, this morning I couldn't sleep so I tossed and turned for almost 2 hours. I decided to go smoke a cigarette and so I grabbed my phone. As soon as I grabbed it, literally I touched it and I got your text at 6:06 a.m. I just came out to smoke and it's 66 degrees out here. Crazy way to start the day. My back is sore today."

We talked about getting tattoos and he had decided on one he would get to honor his two high school friends who died.

10:31 a.m.

"I can go back to the Rehab, IOP and do family day still"

Heather and Jeff came over for dinner – with Stephen.

I had an evening appointment – I called Bryan on the way back.

He was crying and a little hard to understand – he said he hasn't slept much in the past two to three days – he said his back has hurt so much and he just wants to use again, to feel better – he may have used – I think he said Percocet – crying going back to PHP.

Well…he is safe, still, will it last?

I feel so sad that he continues to struggle, and I don't know how to help…

Tuesday March 14, 2017

BLIZZARD

I had a 10 a.m. appointment – snow had just started by the end.

We rested – caught up on shows.

A little anxious – did Bryan go to the hospital?

3:56 p.m. – call

"Hi, Mom! I'm here."

Did he just go to PHP?

Are they going to let him stay?

He called with his case manager, and we talked about family weekend.

"I love you, Mom."

My friend got stuck in our driveway on her way home from work… she stayed the rest of the night in our spare bedroom.

Wednesday March 15, 2017

Had breakfast – Stephen cleared the driveway and my friend left.

I did some work, saw some clients in the afternoon.

NOTHING

Thursday March 16, 2017

Stephen's Birthday.

I forgot!!!

I worked at my part-time job.

I called him from work and apologized so much...I picked up dinner and he cooked.

Heather and Jeff came over, and we chatted and had ice cream, sang "Happy Birthday."

NOTHING

Friday March 17, 2017

I woke up at 4 a.m.

I packed more – got ready for work and then the trip.

I had three clients, and they were good appointments.

My flight left for Florida at 2:00. I talked to the counselor to confirm the family day session. They did not want Bill there.

Went to dinner with Stephen, and we walked down to the beach... it was nice. We had a nice, relaxing evening.

NOTHING

Saturday March 18, 2017

I had a terrible night's sleep. There were noisy neighbors at the hotel, and I barely got any sleep. I woke up exhausted and anxious for the day.

Family Day.

In the morning, it was a group with the family only and there were six client's family members there.

From New York, Florida, New Hampshire, Maine.

It was an intense morning but mostly good – the facilitator is excellent.

The clients arrived about 11:45, and then we had lunch together.

In the afternoon we were all together in the room. Bryan is feeling a little different this time – he was willing before but now feels humbled by almost dying.

> People have told him that he is not committed to treatment. His response is, "I'm just not talking much. Last time, I talked a lot, but it wasn't all real. I have learned a lot, but I still haven't learned to apply it all."

I felt happy, sad, anxious, confused, and cautiously optimistic. We went out to dinner together and then sat in a park.

Sunday March 19, 2017

Met Catherine for coffee.

I am feeling really overwhelmed by this whole addiction thing.

> "I'm tired of only talking about addiction."

I appreciate and respect all those who are doing something to address addiction and help.

> "I'm gonna get through this part (PHP) and take things slow – cause last time I think I tried to do too much too fast. I don't want to die."

Stephen and I brought lunch to Bryan – sat for a little over an hour with him. Stephen did a little Reiki on him. I showed him the EMDR Thera tappers and talked about how it works.

It was a short visit – sad to leave him.

Will I see him again?

Stephen and I got dinner and birthday dessert. Had a nice evening.

Monday March 20, 2017

I got up and went to the beach for sunrise.

We watched the birds.

The flight left at 10 – we got home about 2:15.

I had a client at 5:00 p.m.

I was exhausted.

Settled back at home knowing he's far away.

A death in our community, someone close to someone I know – very heavy heart.

Hoping that won't ever happen to us.

NOTHING

Tuesday March 21, 2017

I woke up tired – had six client appointments.

One of my client's boyfriends died – overdosed.

I love my job and have faith in people's ability to heal and move forward. I will keep doing what I can.

7:34 p.m.

> "I'm gonna talk to the counselor and see if I can get out
> of here and move on soon. These kids here don't even
> understand, they're all worried about pairing up
> – I gotta move on. I know what I have to do."

I am worried about him. He says he knows what he sounds like, but he also knows what's inside him.

I feel like my hesitancy to have full faith in him is hurtful to him. :(

Wednesday March 22, 2017

Stephen worked – I had five appointments through the day.

I felt unsettled, anxious that Bryan may be gearing up to leave where he is.

I know he is struggling; I know I can't do anything… the fear creeps in, the anticipation of what will happen next can be unbearable.

I kept it mostly at bay – but was aware of it.

Always on guard – I have had people say, "You can't live like that." … I wish it were that simple or easy.

NOTHING

Thursday March 23, 2017

I worked at the IOP. I had a couple of no-shows.

I talked to the counselor – she is concerned about Bryan – he is angry and wants to go to IOP – he doesn't like any of the solutions being offered/suggested. She said he has gotten increasingly worse over the week.

I worried about Bryan – angry at his dad for modeling some of the behaviors I see being perpetuated.

Angry at myself for not fighting for him more – though I do know it may not have made any difference.

He was going to call at night….no call.

NOTHING

Friday March 24, 2017

I had five appointments scheduled for the day.

I emailed his counselor to see if we could talk with him together.

The treatment center called – he sounded much better.

The counselor challenged him to see if he was just saying what people wanted to hear.

I'm continuing to try to stay optimistic.

He said he will be in PHP for about two more weeks, then go to IP – he feels good he said.

More and longer periods of time I feel less anxious.

We talked about medical and dental needs. He said he was going to be applying for food stamps again.

Saturday March 25, 2017

Stephen and I had a nice outing doing some shopping, had lunch – and visited Heather at the Humane Society.

Rested in the afternoon – really tired.

My friend texted me in the morning to tell me her daughter had overdosed in their house. She was okay, but my friend is so upset and tired of it all.

Bryan called – they had been at the beach – played basketball – he said he was careful not to run too much – he doesn't want any injuries.

He asked if had I heard from his dad – I said no. He has his family visiting from New York – Bryan said, "He must be stressed." I said, "I've known him for 30 years, and I think he likes it that way…he does not seem to have done much to change it." He laughed… "Yeah."

I slept well.

Sunday March 26, 2017

Cycle for Addiction Awareness

Fundraiser: Reiki/massage.

A few people came – we made a few dollars.

I submitted a press release to several newspapers – one said they will run the story – five others to hear from.

I rested in the evening.

Ready for a busy week ahead.

NOTHING

Monday March 27, 2017

I had a conversation with a client – two clients – about the insanity of addiction, from both sides.

I have learned a lot – feel humbled by the power this has had on so many people.

Increased gratitude that my son is still alive.

I wonder if I will ever be sitting in anyone's office crying about losing him.

I try not to stay there too long – but the thought goes through my mind.

Dinner with Heather and Jeff.

Did Angel card readings.

NOTHING

Tuesday March 28, 2017

I did Reiki on myself when I woke up.

My friend texted me to call her – 5:30 a.m., I called.

Kind of an Alanon 12th step call – support for her that her daughter is in active addiction.

I did meditation, manifesting, with Stephen.

Had lunch with a friend. We talked about a lot of issues. She is very supportive of our efforts.

Bryan called in the evening – he sounded good – said he has a good group of friends who he is with now.

Wednesday March 29, 2017

I had five appointments during the day.

I have an interview scheduled with the newspaper for Friday.

Mostly calm – not anxious – doing my thing, trusting that he is doing his.

Grateful today.

NOTHING

Thursday March 30, 2017

Went to Lewiston.

Saw five clients.

Bill called twice.

Finally, we talked, and he talked about the same stuff as always… worries. He talked about the 'what- ifs', other friends of Bryan, a lot of doom and gloom. Victim stance talk…it's hard to have these discussions when we are not always at the same place.

I told him he should find his own counselor.

He hung up on me – now I worry – will he tell Bryan? Uggghhhh…

He was supposed to call…he didn't.

Did he talk to his dad?

Did he not want to talk to me?

NOTHING

Friday March 31, 2017

I had a few clients in the morning.

He called with his counselor today – I asked why he didn't call yesterday – he said he had been thinking of coming to Maine, but he didn't want to say it before he had fully decided – but then he realized he has support there in Florida. He is going to stay.

A bit anxious, trying to keep it in check – I can't control...so many things...

I told him that I want to change some of the family dynamics and can't talk to his dad – I feel like he is not helpful to the situation. He did not like that – he talked about how it had been a part of his manipulating.

I felt nervous saying this – that the changes I am proposing will make it too hard for him. But I truly believe it's best. Nothing changes if nothing changes.

April 2017

Saturday April 1, 2017

SNOW.....UGGHH!

Went for a walk – have to prepare for our big bike ride.

There was a small article posted in the paper about our fundraising bike ride, we shared it on Facebook.

I am feeling anxious for the release – trying to stay positive and offer hope.

> He called early evening – said he had a good day
> – he is nervous for leaving but is making
> plans for going to HWH – getting a job.

I talked about plans for the future – coming up north for a visit – graduation, birthday, tattoos, visiting the graves of high school friends, family for anniversary.

Talked about Vivitrol and him getting a counselor.

Sunday April 2, 2017

Going to Alanon this morning.

Went – it was a great meeting and it felt so good to be there.

Went for coffee after with a woman I had invited to go – it was good to be out and feel a little social.

Relaxed with Stephen and did some reading.

NOTHING

Monday April 3, 2017

I had coffee with a new friend. Then did some work in the office.

I talked to the director at my part-time job about the Family Program.

I heard from my billing agency; I was selected to do a presentation at the Consortium about ACOA's.

I had two client appointments and they were good appointments.

I got a call from the family counselor.

She wanted to find out what was going on with Bill and Bryan – she is very concerned about their relationship and how co-dependent it is.

An issue arose with the Facebook site – one of my friends questioned me about a post I did about our bike ride. I was very upset.

I had dinner with Heather and Jeff – we had a mini meeting, reading from Alanon literature.

I was so anxious about Bryan leaving for HWH.

Tuesday April 4, 2017

My Facebook post got approved – I felt validated.

I prepared for four appointments and keeping my head straight for whatever happens with Bryan.

Praying for recovery.

I was anxious waiting, still worrying about our family dynamic and his father.

I called him in the afternoon – I was a little short with him – felt left out. He said he had tried to call. He said he felt good physically and emotionally – has a good roommate, and he is excited to get on with his life. He said he's going to get the Vivitrol shot.

I felt bad after talking to him – I am hopeful again – trying to be realistic about all the possibilities…and will continue with my life.

Wednesday April 5, 2017

I had five appointments spread throughout the day.

7:37 a.m.

Bryan called – sounds good.

He texted at night – he was at dinner with friends.

Thursday April 6, 2017

I called a friend and caught up from last months. Worked at IOP. I saw four clients.

Text in a.m.:

9:37 a.m.

We are starting to plan for him to come up in nine weeks.

From the book, *Law of Attraction:*

It was a passage that talked about paying attention to the signs that are being sent from the Universe guiding every aspect of life. It talked about paying attention to your thoughts and feelings and recognizing how they are impacting outcomes.

I called on the way home from work – no answer – no return call… yet…(one hour later)

"Let him live his life…don't worry unless there's a reason…don't jump to any conclusions."

6:30 p.m.

He called: "Hi Mom – I'm at the Center – sorry I didn't call. I forgot so wanted to call you quick – don't want to worry you. I'm at group. I love you."

Relief – frustration that I don't stay in faith.

Friday April 7, 2017

I had a couple of clients and then a couple canceled.

I got my notes done and faxed in.

> He sent me a passage from the *Law of Attraction* calendar
> that I gave him…he said it was fitting for the texts he
> woke up to – his friend got kicked out of a HWH
> – homeless again.

> The quote was right on the theme of this; it was about
> gratitude for what you have and how that can be helpful
> in moving forward into a new journey. There was also a
> suggestion for developing new skills
> to accomplish goals on the new path.

It was a good day.

Feeling content, happy, and productive, and forward with optimism.

Saturday April 8, 2017

I did yoga, walked the dogs.

I did some work on the presentation and an online training.

> He was going to a memorial service
> on the beach for a friend of his.

Stephen and I relaxed/snoozed in the afternoon.

Went to dinner and to an evening workshop that included a lot
of meditation.

Bryan told me to call after – 8:30.

I called three times, went to voicemail each time. I was instantly
upset and anxious. Did he leave?

What's happening?

8:59 p.m. – "So....you told me to call, phone goes straight to VM, you're not answering my message...you knew when I was going to be calling. Please let me know something."

Can I handle it?

What should I prepare for?

9:06 p.m.

"Phone died, call me?"

When I finally talked to him, he said that a lot of people in the house are relapsing, so he stayed away.

Sunday April 9, 2017

I walked the dogs in the morning.

Went to an Alanon meeting and then for coffee and bought some crystals at a friend's store.

I came home – I did a bike ride.

He sent me texts from the *Law of Attraction*
– from Saturday –

A quote that was about being moved toward great things
no matter how difficult it might be; a reminder that
happiness is dependent on us.

We prepared for a Full Moon meditation.

Did our meditation for the Full Moon – expected a few people to join – no one showed up.

Sat by the fire pit – Shannon stopped by, and we had a nice visit.

We talked about scheduling/booking flights for him to come up to Massachusetts in eight weeks.

Monday April 10, 2017

Did yoga, walked the dogs.

Went for a ten-mile bike ride – felt good!

I saw one client and had one cancellation.

Bryan said he did some dog-sitting for someone.

They started doing our driveway.

Feeling mostly settled and confident about how Bryan is doing.

He sounded good.

Gratitude was the message from the *Law of Attraction.*

Heather and Jeff came for dinner.

Tuesday April 11, 2017

Day two of the driveway.

He sent me the *Law of Attraction* reading; your life is a reflection of what is inside.

Went for a bike ride – third day in a row. Training for Addiction Awareness ride.

2:32 p.m.

"Someone stole my tablet. I'm done. I'm gonna flip!"

Felt content, happy.

Had afternoon appointments.

After reading this – he had also been talking to his dad about it – his dad yelled at him…has been spending more time with him.

I hear his commitment to his recovery cracking. Slipping back to thinking he doesn't really need groups or meeting – just his dad.

I feel discouraged and sick.

Wednesday April 12, 2017

Texted a little in the a.m. - I had some appointments - he was going to a noon meeting.

> "I tried to get kicked out last night – I didn't go
> back to the house – didn't want to get high."

I called in the afternoon – he sounds more and more unsettled; he said, "I just want to be home. I don't want to just sleep in a bed – I want a home."

The only home he has or knows right now is his dad's – he has not ever been able to stay clean there – but at the same time it offers him the comfort of the memory of being a kid.

> 4:18 p.m. – text

> "Another friend dead."

> He didn't go to group – talked to his counselor
> and they scheduled a 1:1 for Thursday.

I talked to the family counselor who agrees that the more time they spend together, the unhealthier it is for Bryan.

> He texted later – he went out to play pool with friends.
> He was going to call his sponsor.

> He didn't get the Vivitrol shot – he thought
> he was kicked out.

I am sad, sick, scared – don't know if I will see him in eight weeks.

Thursday April 13, 2017

Went to my part time job to work, had six clients scheduled, four ended up coming.

Talked to Bryan; he said he was waiting to hear from IOP if he could go back or not.

It turned out, he knew he was not going back – he had been staying at his dad's and didn't tell me because he didn't want me to freak out on his dad.

6:29 p.m. – I texted:

"I hate that you lied to me and then avoid me, and I hate your disease that lies to you. I feel sick and my heart hurts and I'm afraid for your life. Based on your actions, not your words."

7:41 p.m. – text

"I just saw this; I was playing basketball. I'm sorry."

11:22 p.m. – text

"I got a new sponsor. His name is Paul. I'm gonna do whatever he asks. I just talked to him."

Friday April 14, 2017

Walked the dogs.

Had a few appointments during the day.

Keeping my focus on me, my life, my other family members, and trying to manage my own emotions.

I told him – I will not buy him plane tickets to come to Massachusetts in June until he pays me back for HWH rent. I paid for two weeks, he only stayed one; he said he would.

He was supposed to meet with sponsor, but his sponsor had to work.

Feeling prepared for a downward turn…but also believe he is capable of accomplishing any positive thing he wants.

Saturday April 15, 2017

Walked at the golf course with dogs.

Texted briefly in the a.m. with Bryan. He was going to be meeting with his sponsor.

8:12 p.m.

"Hope you had a good day. Love you!"

"I did. love you too so much."

Sunday April 16, 2017

Easter

Rested.

Went for a bike ride.

6:07 p.m. – text

"I'm ok. I just don't want to be in PSL anymore. Just the community here, I'm done with it."

7:49 p.m.

"Can I drive to Maine?"

10:00 p.m. – Catherine sent me a text message. She wanted to tell me about a girl who is staying with him that Bill is trying to help.

11:00 – Text from her: "Call me in the morning, we urgently need to talk."

Monday April 17, 2017

Heather's birthday!!!

Bryan decided that he was going to come to Maine.

I had some appointments during the day.

There was a lot of talk about if Bryan was going to come to Maine.

There was drama in Florida with Bill and another girl who had stayed with him.

Had a great dinner and celebration with Heather and Jeff for her birthday.

9:19 p.m.

"I'm about to leave mothership."

Anxious, excited, surprised Bryan is coming.

Tuesday April 18, 2017

I woke up to see on Facebook… "A rough start leaving FL."

I texted him at 6 a.m. – he was stopped at Denny's for breakfast. He checked in at the restaurant – still in Florida – only a few hours from his dad's.

10:29 a.m.

"Mom, I don't think it's safe, but I can't even drive. I need to go to sleep. I just went to Burger King, and they told me I need to be careful; this is horrible. I'm like seeing double. I'm pulling up right now; call me when you can.

I booked a hotel, and he was able to check in early.

He had definitely been using the whole time – very unsafe – I was a wreck – but had to work…I prayed a lot.

11:27 a.m.

"I'm in the room mother."

Wednesday April 19, 2017

He got up early – started driving.

I worked, did my best to focus on that.

Made it from Maryland to New Jersey.

I felt relieved that he made that kind of progress.

Held my breath all day.

Thursday April 20, 2017

Went to my part- time job.

Saw one client, two others canceled.

Bryan asked me to Western Union him some money.

There was a problem with the Western Union kiosk. He was with a friend, and they left while waiting for the machine to reset.

I called back to check – he had just gotten stopped by the police.

They arrested him for possession of heroin.

He got released, I booked a hotel; he was too tired to drive.

He was out and about, getting high – lost his wallet. He didn't get checked into the hotel until 11:00 p.m.

I was so worried, anxious, and scared. I didn't know if he would live or if he would die.

Friday April 21, 2017

I woke up at 3:15 a.m. I couldn't go back to sleep. I decided to get up. I was going to New Jersey to get Bryan.

I woke Stephen up to ask if he would go with me.

We left at 4 a.m.

Couldn't contact Bryan at the hotel – his phone rang, he didn't answer or respond to texts.

Stephen called the room phone and he answered. If that hadn't worked, I was going to call for a wellness check…I thought he might have died in the room.

We were going to have him meet us in Connecticut. Then he asked if we could meet him in Yonkers – THEN – he was too 'out of it' and we ended up driving to New Jersey.

We picked him up, after we traveled eight and a half hours, then headed back to Maine – he slept most of the way – got home at 10:15 p.m.

Exhausted, relieved, and anxious.

Saturday April 22, 2017

I was so tired and woke up about 6:30 a.m.

Rested all day – did some shopping with Bryan for food.

Talked to my family – Thank God they were supportive.

Anxious, tired, hopeful, happy to have a little bit of time with him – no one knows the future. I will cherish this time.

Bryan lost another friend from treatment.

I showed him my office; he didn't really know what I do – seemed to be impressed. I realized how much he doesn't know me or my life.

Sad about losing another friend.

Sunday April 23, 2017

I woke up about 6:00 – had a good night's rest.

Did a few things in the morning – had lunch – walked the dogs.

Did work for my job.

It was nice to see Bryan. We talked a bit about expectations and goals.

Culture shock, struggle, and stress.

He needs to replace his license and get a social security card – before he can get a job.

"I made it through another day."

"I feel more stuck now than ever, due to my own actions."

He will work with Stephen to 'pay off' $200 debt, $10 per hour.

I visited Heather.

I know he doesn't like being here -– he misses all his friends – on the phone constantly. But I am trying to appreciate him being here.

Monday April 24, 2017

I walked the dogs.

> He worked with Stephen scraping house paint.

Showered.

> Tired, long day, arms hurt.

> Took a nap.

I had six clients throughout the day.

> Felt good. I did a good job and then had family dinner
> …that was nice.

I picked Bryan up at the house.

I noticed that I am focused on my life – trusting he will figure out his.

Tuesday April 25, 2017

I had two clients.

I walked in between the rain – walked the dogs in the morning.

> He relaxed – watched Netflix.

> Took a nap – "When I woke up, I found out my friend died.
> I was just talking to him…"

> "I was just sad….it makes me think about having a
> purpose to be here – I've been close and I'm still here…"

> Got to sleep – finished Suboxone taper – detox is over.

Looking forward to getting detox completely done and over with.

It felt good to catch up on work. Co-existing with Bryan on new and different terms.

Wednesday April 26, 2017

Had a meeting with Bryan and a guy who is the head of a Maine recovery organization.

He talked to Bryan about the same stuff – Stephen and I went shopping.

Had two afternoon appointments.

Got dinner ready.

Brought Bryan to a SMART recovery meeting.

It was different/interesting going to the SMART recovery meeting.

I was asked to be on the Board of Directors for a non-profit organization for Addiction Recovery.

Thursday April 27, 2017

I went to Lewiston – got there, no computer in my office.

I saw five or six clients – they didn't all stay for the full hour. It was frustrating.

> Bryan finished a Suboxone taper – said he would be sick – he was a bit tired but did not seem very sick.

2:30 a.m. – woke up – heard a great horned owl outside, loud and several hoots…striking.

Friday April 28, 2017

I had a few clients scheduled throughout the day.

I was tired – talked to boss from the IOP – told him I did not want to work there anymore. It was a conversation that did not go well; I was stressed out with the situation with Bryan, and people were not showing up for sessions at the IOP, and the communication was not great there. I should have given more notice, but I could not tolerate it. I felt bad, but I also knew that something had to give, and I could not do it.

> He went with Stephen and painted for three hours.

> He was on his phone this whole time.

He periodically said things about various
options of places he could go in Florida.

I left my computer for Bryan to use to apply for jobs – he said, "I
will Mom, I have all weekend to do it."

By about 9-10 p.m., he was telling me he was going back to
Florida – he didn't want to be here – he said he never wanted
to really come here to stay. He said he makes those kinds of
decisions when he is high.

I was very upset and confused – had a hard time falling asleep –
heard two owls that night again; a bard owl and great horned owl.

Saturday April 29, 2017

Woke him up about 8:15 a.m.

He admitted that he intentionally doesn't put effort
in to doing more for himself.

We talked on and off all day about his 'plan' – we were at odds.
It was so reminiscent of our relationship.

I felt resentful because I felt like he was going to want to hang
around for another week and have me drive him down and back
to court, and I was mad.

"I'm sorry, Mom. I always do this and make impulsive
decisions when I'm high, and then I regret them.
I don't want to be in Maine – I'm not comfortable here."

I was so sad that he didn't want to stay, and I am so afraid that
he won't get the help he needs before he dies.

He left about 4:00 p.m.

Texted about 12:20 a.m. that he had arrived in New York at his
friend's house.

Sunday April 30, 2017

I had quite a difficult first half of the day – I could not stop crying

– on and off – most of the morning.

Grief and loss.

Went grocery shopping.

Rested.

Watched TV

Did some work for my job.

6:19 p.m. – text

"I'm sorry things weren't different. I love you.
I don't intend to hurt you.

I love you. I'm not giving up. I'm sorry I hurt you so much.
It kills me. It really does. I'm sorry. I seriously feel just
horrible. I don't want to go through this again. Although
you may not think it affects me, it does a lot. Yesterday
was very tough on me. I don't know if I've ever
felt so low before."

Texted with Bryan a bit – made some peace, shared some empathy, sorrow, compassion, and forgiveness for each other's side of the struggle.

May 2017

Monday May 1, 2017

Settling in with the idea of Bryan not being here.

The space in my heart and our home is being filled back in.

Saw clients, did some paperwork, and had some rest in the middle of the day.

Late afternoon had a frustrating conversation with him.

He went to dinner at his sister's house and saw niece and nephew.

Then had a real nice dinner with Heather and Jeff.

11:53 p.m. – Facebook post:

"Bye FL, think it's time to move on for good.
This feels right. I love you all down there.
Thank y'all for everything."

Tuesday May 2, 2017

We texted early a.m. I told him I thought it was a good idea to be in New York with his friend. He was surprised.

Maybe this is IT.

Action not Hope.

He texted about his plans to apply for insurance and food stamps.

I felt so happy – he sounds confident and committed.

Later that night there was a question of where he had been out, and car battery died – his father thought he was buying drugs in Utica.

I paused, questioned – who to believe?

I want to believe in Bryan.

Wednesday May 3, 2017

Walked the dogs.

1:17 p.m.

"I finally feel like I'm where I need to be."

Had five appointments through the day.

Texted with Bryan – he sounds good – made a lot of arrangements for doctor appointments.

Goes to court on Friday in New Jersey – his friend that he lives with is going with him.

3:19 p.m.

"Thank you for sticking by me. I'm grateful for it.
I can't wait to see you in a month."

Thursday May 4, 2017

Went to the agency to finish my notes before leaving there for good. It was not working for me; too much for me to manage at this time.

Heather and I then went to the beach. We walked for one and a half hours – went to lunch.

Saw about a dozen eagles feeding at a marsh – watched for about half an hour.

4:10 p.m.

"This has been a long day. We've been busy getting
stuff done. Been a long but productive week."

Bryan spent a few hours with his friend at the doctor – they were afraid something was really wrong – turns out he has migraines.

They left about 9 p.m. for NJ – he had court in the morning – they apparently got in about 1-2 a.m.

Friday May 5, 2017

He was up early – after a few hours of sleep – got to court – 8:30 – and he called me ten minutes later.

9:10 a.m.

"I'm so happy right now. Things worked out how they were supposed to. I love you, Mom."

They dropped the felony charge – but he has to go back on 5-23-17 and take care of a traffic issue or something.

1:47 p.m.

"We're home mom. Taking a nap, call ya later."

I had a few clients.

Felt relieved about his court situation. Grateful his friend went with him.

I continue to pray – there are so many things he needs help with: problem-solving, dealing with feelings.

Saturday May 6, 2017

Stephen and I went to a spirit festival – we had a table there for our Wellness Center.

Bryan called in the a.m. to say his phone is dying – won't hold a charge. He was very frustrated sounding…

"Why is everything going wrong?!"

I encouraged him to hang in there – because I believe he can figure it out – life will always have ups and downs.

A little nervous about his ability to manage stress – without using drugs.

Later he called and said that his phone was okay
– the cats kept unplugging the cord.

I had a reading from one of the vendors – one of the things she saw was a coin – like quarter sized…I pray it will be a one-year coin someday.

Sunday May 7, 2017

Walked the dogs.

Went for a bike ride.

Rested.

Snacked.

Made a grocery list.

Stayed home, played play station.

Minimal contact.

Mostly peaceful.

Monday May 8, 2017

8:50 a.m.

"Car won't start"

8:55 a.m.

"Terrible…I got appointments at 11 and 2"

9:03 a.m.

"This is awful"

9:05 a.m.

"You will get through it… build the muscles for life…patience, acceptance, flexibility, perseverance…use gratitude and prayer, you'll be fine."

9:06 a.m.

"I know, I'm doing that, I am."

The car started – was able to reschedule his appointment until later in the day – car fixed.

I got teary toward the end of our conversation.

I felt relieved and realized I had been holding my breath… "What will happen next?'"

12:36 p.m.

"Were you tearing up on the phone?"

12:37 p.m.

"Yes…. relief, gratitude, and pride."

"Fair enough…I love you."

Tuesday May 9, 2017

Mindfulness practice.

Walked dogs.

Had a 9:00 appointment.

Went for a bike ride.

Anxious not hearing from Bryan – having some concerns about his commitment and motivation. I had a thought that it may be slipping because he does not have a penalty or felony over his head right now.

He called about 12:15, said he has a job interview. He did express a concern about its location. He wanted me to know where the program is that he is going to.

12:20 p.m. – text

"I'm not gonna go to that interview, it's too far. Sometimes not jumping into stuff and being patient is the best option."

I feel better, relieved, for now.

Wednesday May 10, 2017

Walked the dogs in the a.m.

I had five appointments throughout the day.

Talked to Bryan during the day – he said he had considered coming to surprise me for Mother's Day – but it would cost too much.

I thanked him for the thought – it meant a lot.

He is supposed to be starting a program that will be a Suboxone program with counseling.

Still sounds committed; I am still cautiously optimistic.

Thursday May 11, 2017

Had some appointments and supervision/consultation.

10:55 a.m.

"Going to my appointment now. Can you help with copay if needed, mother?"

(Of course, I said yes!)

Post on Facebook that I didn't understand.

Everything okay?

What happened?

6:55 p.m.

"Yeah, I'm fine. Nothing, I don't want to talk about it. It's not bad."

Friday May 12, 2017

I did a two-hour presentation for counselors and case managers about Adult Children of Alcoholics. I feel that not enough clinicians are aware of the significant impact this has on folks.

It went pretty well – I got a parking ticket.

11:45 a.m. text

"Hope you're doing well…I will call you later"

11:47 p.m.

"I'm not. I'll be ok though. I love you."

???

"I'm ok mom. Love you."

"I love you. I'm ok. I don't have to use over this. I didn't. I feel better. I'll be ok."

"I know you will."

Saturday May 13, 2017

Stephen and I went to a wellness fair.

4:29 p.m. text –

"I'm happy people are proud, but I just wish this industry would change."

I called and asked if he would be willing or able to come to Massachusetts for Mother's Day…we offered to help with gas and tolls.

Sunday May 14, 2017

MOTHER'S DAY

We went to West Springfield, had lunch with Alec, Beth, and Bryan.

Bryan drove from New York to Massachusetts.

"Finally, words are starting to match up with my actions."

Went to the cemetery before going back.

"I'm happy I'm here and not there… I very easily could have been where they are."

Monday May 15, 2017

Had a few clients.

12:13 p.m.

"I love you."

Did some work.

1:51 p.m.

"I got food stamps."

Went and signed papers for the Board Member position.

Happy…proud…he is taking care of his own needs

Tuesday May 16, 2017

Walked the dogs.

Worked.

> "I got my medical stuff set up, food stamps, got my license back and went to one court date. I almost accomplished everything I set out to do. Now I have to get a job."

Meditated.

Honestly – I am finding myself just going through my days – not so anxious about what he's doing – living the way life should be… not over involved, loving from a distance.

Wednesday May 17, 2017

Yoga

I made a video for Cycle for Addiction Awareness.

A big treatment center/sober living home homeowner in Florida got sentenced today – it was a very big deal. He was charged and convicted of insurance fraud, criminal charges having to do with prostitution and maybe kidnapping.

"He got 27.5 years. He deserved that and maybe worse.
I hate him."

1:47 p.m.

"It's some ugly stuff he did. I cannot express the immense gratitude and relief I have that you are away from that…it is so much
better. I hope you feel the same. I know you miss some people
and worry about Becky still…"

2:02 p.m.

"I am too. I've thought about the Becky situation
– I don't miss her; I miss the idea.
She did nothing positive for me but leave me with Hep C."

"Just keep taking care of yourself and doing what you're doing,
and the rest will come."

"I know it will; I'm starting to see that and more."

Thursday May 18, 2017

Rode bike ten miles.

Kayaked with Heather.

9:06 a.m.

"Good morning. Grateful to wake up today and be functioning. I love you. I hope you have a great day."

Went to the water with Stephen.

Practiced Reiki with Stephen.

1:44 p.m. – text

"2 and ½ weeks ago I left Maine. You thought it might
be the last time you ever saw me. I could tell by the look
in your eyes, and it killed me. You lost faith, not in me but
in general. I couldn't deal with the awful feeling of putting
you through that anymore. I could have gone one of two
ways: give up to not feel or fight through it.

I chose the better option. When times are hard, I
remember the look in your eyes, the pain and scare
I put you through. Giving up and dying is not an option
for me now. Some days are hard but it's part of the
process. The joy in your voice and through your texts are
what I'm living for. The happiness and peace that you
and Dad have now make me want to keep going and not
give up. I'm not perfect, no one is, but I'm going to strive
to be great. I'm going to use the tools you gave me from
birth as well as the tools dad has given me. I'm going to
make a difference one day. I don't know how, but I know
I will. All of this takes patience as well as willingness
to deal with the negatives that come along with living
a normal life. I'm not clean off of drugs
because of me, it's because of us.

We did this together and will continue. I love you more than
words can describe. This is your Mother's Day card.
Thank you for being perfect, even if your imperfections are
perfect to me. I love you. Thank you."

Talked with Bryan – text made me so happy.

Saw two clients.

"I can hear the joy and peace in your voice.
There's no gift I can give you that will match that."

1:50 p.m.

"Thank you….and it's such a gift to yourself. Times like these I
struggle to find sufficient words to match the depth of joy and
gratitude for you in my life. I hear the change in your words and
the conviction in your voice. You will continue to make a positive
impact in this world…I love you so much."

A blessed day – JUST FOR TODAY.

Heather and Jeff had some drama in the evening; he was threat-
ening her …we went over.

Friday May 19, 2017

I had a couple of morning appointments.

Exhausted and discouraged about other family member's issues.

Saturday May 20, 2017

Fifteen-mile bike ride in the morning.

Stephen and I were at a Holistic Fair with our Wellness Center.

Had a good day.

10:17 a.m.

"Good morning. I love you."

11:22 a.m.

"Good morning mothership. I love you!!!"

We both are just 'doing our thing'… working things out. So little worry, much less worry.

Will it last?

He sounds so confident and sure.

We talked about tattoo planning.

He started talking about planning a birthday dinner – he asked one of his grandmothers to come and she said yes.

Sunday May 21, 2017

Drove down to Massachusetts.

He asked if I wanted to invite my mom and sister to his birthday dinner –– I told him it was his dinner…we just can't pay for everyone.

I had lunch and dinner with my mother and sister; we shopped for plants, and they helped me with buying plants. I asked them if they wanted to come to his birthday; neither gave a definite answer. My mother actually cited an argument between her and Bryan that had taken place two years prior as a reason she didn't want to go.

7:15 p.m.

"What if I went to NJ to stay tomorrow night and drive back Tuesday night?"

"Then you would be hanging around outside the hotel from 11:15 when you have court…but you could…it's up to you."

"Never mind."

Tuesday May 22, 2017

Drove home from Massachusetts.

He said he got a job interview and that he has allergies.

Went shopping with Stephen for mulch and other gardening stuff.

6:56 p.m.

"Hope you had a good day. When you get a chance, send something for the book?"

"It was extremely stressful. I'm trying not to flip out; I'm angry."

Worried…can he handle the stress?!

10:52 p.m. – Facebook:

"Ima keep building off this. It may not seem like a lot but a month without using (outside of rehab) for this guy right here is an accomplishment. T.Y. to my friend and family who have and continue to support me. Love you guys."

Relieved – sounds like he is staying focused.

Tuesday May 23, 2017

Twenty-mile bike ride with Stephen.

I had tried to talk to him in the evening, and he said that he and his friend were still out at dinner.

> He drove to New Jersey for court.
>
> Met a friend and went to dinner.
>
> He said that his friend said that the hotel
> he is staying in is a crack hotel.

I started getting worried and a funny feeling... lingering fears of the past. He sent me a picture of the TV in the hotel room when he got in there.

I felt slightly better seeing that, but still anxious.

Wednesday May 24, 2017

Got up early – went and rented a truck to move the remaining stuff from the house (the old one).

Heather and Jeff met us there.

> He called about 10:30 a.m. – He went the wrong direction
> leaving New Jersey ended up in Pennsylvania
> – got to his doctor appointment slightly late.

We loaded the truck, then went to lunch – unloaded the stuff at our house, then I showered, got ready for two appointments.

Paid co-pay for Bryan to go to the doctor appointment.

Talked to him – he said he had used when he was in New Jersey – he had been so stressed after driving down and going to court. He had been afraid he was going to jail.

He said that he was angry with himself – hates that he disappointed others. He told the doctor and will get back on track.

I hate that I feel like I contributed some to this. Rented a shitty hotel for him and then stressed about it via text last night.

But grateful he sounds like he is back on track and not letting it get him down too much.

Thursday May 25, 2017

Went for a 15-mile bike ride at 6:00 with Stephen.

Had two clients.

Did notes.

Planted plants.

1:00 p.m.

Talked to him briefly – he went to the doctor to get set up on Suboxone program.

Did some work.

Held off calling to 'give him space.'

He called at 7:30.

He got approved for Medicaid.

Has an abscess.

Friday May 26, 2017

I had an 8, 11, 12, and 2:00 appointments.

He was able to get hold of Stephen to get information and so was able to get prescription for Suboxone.

Bryan had a doctor appointment in the a.m. – I had to leave my appointment to pay his co-pay.

During appointment, he texted because he didn't have prescription information.

His thoughts for today:

4:48 p.m.

Relief

Accomplished

Proud

Grateful for Stephen

(Becky called me)

Confused

Sad

So many different emotions.

Heartbroken

So many different emotions.

Saturday May 27, 2017

I drove with Stephen to Millinocket to map out the big bike ride we are planning.

I was reminded of the last time I was there – Bryan went to jail.

We rested in the afternoon.

Sat by the fire with Heather for a couple hours at night.

Felt relaxed – so much less stress about Bryan.

There is always a vague 'knowing' that things can change in an instant – I always feel prepared or like I need to be.

10:29 p.m.

Words for the day:

> "Um. . Video. Games are fun and cat peed all over
> my clothes so annoyed. I can't wait for two weeks!"

Sunday May 28, 2017

Stephen and I went on a 15-mile bike ride.

Then came home and spent several hours working in the yard.

Bryan called in between – he is still stressed about his clothes getting peed on. Needed somewhere to put his clothes – we had a miscommunication/misunderstanding.

There is still mistrust between us, him feeling like I think he's 'bad' or like he's always being treated badly.

2:12 p.m.

"It sounded like you were annoyed by something when I called…I felt like you were projecting on me. I was asking. That's why I don't like asking for things."

I think we worked it out – but I have a feeling he is struggling a lot.

Nothing I can do.

Monday May 29, 2017

Stephen and I got up and did an early meditation.

I did a phone consult for work.

We went to Home Depot, Stephen got stuff for work – we got some outdoor stuff.

Walmart – did shopping.

Had a couch – Netflix afternoon – rested.

Texted a little with Bryan…chatted throughout the day.

7:35 p.m.

"I'm tired and am trying to find a way to get by each day. I need to get a job and start moving forward. I feel I can handle that now."

7:36 p.m.

"You are doing it… day by day… :)"

"Rest well and I will talk to you tomorrow if not later."

Tuesday May 30, 2017

Had three appointments during the day.

Did a 15-mile bike ride and felt good about it.

6:59 p.m.

"I have an interview tomorrow, it's a pizza place!"

Still feeling some freedom in this change – freedom to live my life with more joy.

I am trying to stay in the present – mixed feelings of hope and worry. A pizza place was a time in the past where he used.

9:02 p.m.

"Progress not perfection.
In time things will come, with patience."

Wednesday May 31, 2017

Did yoga in the a.m.

Had an early appointment then afternoon appointments.

Bryan and I talked about his interview (pizza place) and our up-coming birthday celebration and tattoos.

When we were talking about birthday celebration he said,
"I'm excited. It's kind of like the excitement
I used to have to go buy drugs."

We decide on tattoos and scheduled them.

He sounds good.

7:30 p.m.

(When asked for words for the book)

"Ummmm nothing really happened today. I'm lonely."

Little niggles of fear creep in daily though they don't accumulate.
Makes me sad and a little worried.

June 2017

Thursday June 1, 2017

Went on a training bike ride.

On FB.....................

11:54 a.m.

"This side is so much better. Thank God for the family and friends I have."

Felt good to be out.

Feeling a little sad for Bryan.

Will he be okay to handle feeling sad and lonely?

It's not up to me.

Friday June 2, 2017

Had two appointments during the day.

10:49 a.m.

"Dear South Florida rehabs. My insurance is up in 5 days. I know I've been a good customer. Now stop fuckin calling me. I don't wanna go to detox at your spa, I'm good. Although Tempurpedic beds, free Newport, ice cream machines and Xbox or PlayStation, back massages, pedicures, acupuncture and other amenities sounds enticing, I'm good. Plus, I'm not using. Y'all got your couple million from my insurance. Other than a few people I know and places I been to that I truly respect, stop. Thank you."

4:30 p.m.

"Feeing blessed. Start new job tomorrow. I'm just getting started. Next up, placement test for college. Grateful every day for this opportunity."

Later in the day a photographer came out.

Relaxed in the evening.

Saturday June 3, 2017

2:14 p.m. – FB

"I just got a message from a random girl. 4 months ago, to-day I overdosed and died. She just told me what happened. I was with 2 people that night. Neither of them helped me. If it wasn't for this random person I would have died on Feb. 3, 2017. Now I'm living a better life than I could have pictured. Thank you, Sharon, for saving my life, while 2 people watched me go lifeless."

10:20 p.m. – Facebook:

"Sooooo today was rather disappointing. I went to work excited and ready to work hard. Come to find out my back-ground check didn't check out. The State of NJ didn't change my felony to a misdemeanor yet and I don't have court till the 27th. Hopefully they give me another chance come Monday. Pray for me please, I really wanted this."

So sad for him. He was embarrassed.

Worried still about emotion management.

Twenty-mile bike ride with Stephen.

Work in yard.

Feeling accomplished.

Sunday June 4, 2017

Stephen and I did a 15-mile ride.

Facebook memory came up 11:51 a.m.

"Bryan and Karen are celebrating 6 years of friendship on Facebook." He wrote:

"I feel like we've been friends for way longer than 6 years, Mom. Well, happy 6 years mother. You're the most amazing woman I know."

Went and did some errands – getting ready to get chickens and the needed supplies.

Stopped at a fundraiser Heather's work held.

Rested – snoozed on the couch for two to three hours.

Meditation at the bonfire – four people showed up.

FB – 7:36 p.m. – Facebook:

He shared a video we had made for our fundraiser bike ride.

"This is something that is so important to my mom and step-dad. These little things can make a difference. I have a lot of friends on here that are involved in programs. Regardless how you feel about me, please listen to this and check out cycle for addiction awareness please. Thank you."

Monday June 5, 2017

One appointment.

Front page of paper about our bike ride!

11:47 a.m.

"I'm proud of you and grateful to call you my mother."

First board meeting.

Dinner with Heather.

Feeling good about where we are – all of us – in our journey.

I chatted with Sharon – the woman who saved Bryan's life.

Some of what she said was, "You have a great son, though he didn't deserve any of that, I give you my word that kid asked me to help him drag Bryan's lifeless body to the grassy ditch. The hardest part was he was blueish and lifeless. I lost his pulse two times...I've never had a guy I never met before be dead in my lap. Then when I found out how young omg...I mean I'm only 28. I hope and pray he stays on the right path like he is; he seems to have a lot of ambition and life, not to mention an amazing loving family."

We talked about this conversation;
he had not realized some of the details of what happened.

Tuesday June 6, 2017

Bryan's birthday!!!

Slept late – he was okay with where he was for his birthday.

26 years old!

I had five appointments during the day.

"Mom, I'm grocery shopping, and I wonder what you want for the room. I want to use my food stamps, and I figured I could help with some stuff."

I did not think he would reach this birthday – really.

He had chicken parmesan with his friend for dinner.

Grateful.

7:47 p.m.

"Going to sleep soon! So excited...one full day of work, then we head to MA! Tattoo, birthday, and graduation plus some good food and pictures!!"

"Yeah, I'm so dams excited too. I can't wait. I love you!"

Wednesday June 7, 2017

Getting ready for long, celebrating weekend.

Saw three clients in the morning.

Went for a 20-mile bike ride.

Two evening clients.

7:53 p.m.

I'm very proud of how you handled the events of the week and your birthday…"

7:55 p.m.

"We planned a trip ahead of time and following through with these things is a good feeling. It's easier on everyone. Being able to contribute with food and little things is a good feeling too."

"I'm more aware of it now than usual."

"You have no idea the many ways this is a big deal!"

Thursday June 8, 2017

Left the house at 10 a.m. and arrived in West Springfield at 2:30.

Went to eat – Alec came over and Bryan came in and ate.

Went to an Alanon meeting.

Went to play basketball – caught up with an old friend.

Picked Beth and Ana up and visited with them at the room.

Saw another friend at her work.

Bryan had gone out – thought he would be back sooner, got anxious.

"Excited about going for tattoo – didn't sleep that well!"

Friday June 9, 2017

Tattoos.

Really happy with the tattoo.

Haircut.

"Found out my friend passed away."

Watched a video of Bryan's friend from high school, who died two years ago yesterday – his sister made it. It was a montage of his photos to the Coldplay song, "Lights will guide you home."

"I am glad I could spend time with friends and family and not worry about my next fix."

FB – 6:05 p.m. Facebook:

"RIP bro. We been friends for a few years now, and you were always there for me when I needed it. You introduced me to Kevin Gates, so whenever I hear him, I'll think about you. Love you bro."

Met with my friend.

Went to dinner.

Two people Bryan knew died yesterday.

One actually had been dead for four days...uggh.

Saturday June 10, 2017

Woke up at 4:30 – Mountain meditation.

"I slept a bit last night."

Did a 25-mile bike ride with Stephen.

Showered.

Birthday dinner with Bryan, Stephen, kids, my stepmother, and two of Bryan's friends came to celebrate with us.

3:23 p.m.

"Actions speak louder than words. Every time. I go to say something, now I check myself."

Nothing from my family – they had been invited, and my sister was very non-committal, and the other, my mother, said she is upset because Bryan 'reemed her out' the last time she saw him. That was two years ago – he was still struggling a bit and has died since then. My resentment is huge.

FB – 9:32 p.m. Facebook:

"Through the tragedy, I'm able to sit back and look at my life and be grateful that I'm spending this weekend with my family, and my two closest friends are clean and sober – I wouldn't be here today if it wasn't for y'all."

Sunday June 11, 2017

Stephen and I walked at the reservoir – I did an early meditation.

Still feeling upset and resentful.

Stephen and I had coffee at 10:00 with friends of ours.

Went to Dunkin Donuts – Bryan worked on a job application.

He gave a Red Bull can and a few dollars to a homeless man.

Graduation.

Lunch.

9:13 p.m. – Facebook message – printed

"I don't say much often about this, but I feel I need to share this. My mom is the most important woman to me in my life, and I love you more than anything. With that being said, I have to say how beyond grateful I am to have a stepfather treat you so well. Through the ups and downs and hell you have gone through during my journey, this man never turned his back on me and never said how shitty of a son I was to you. That's the true definition of love. I see it and I acknowledge it, and I hope to implement it in my life in the future. Stephen, thank you. From the bottom of my heart, thank you for taking care of my mom, loving my mom, and loving me when so many others didn't. I love you. Thank you."

I got really emotional.

Monday June 12, 2017

Lawn mowing.

House cleaning.

> Watched basketball – talking with others on Facebook about the play offs.

Grocery Shopping.

Evening client appointment.

Ice cream with Heather after.

Emotionally tired.

Grateful for this change – we were able to have some conversation about feelings and emotional issues – a relief, I can breathe…

Tuesday June 13, 2017

Walk with dogs.

Morning appointment.

Bryan went to medical doctor to care for some issues – he might have a concussion.

> He said he will be applying for a job later in the day.

We will be going to New Jersey in two weeks for his court case – we talked about needing to plan for that.

I posted about our bike ride on several sites related to addiction – got contacted by the administrator -- my post got deleted. We went back and forth a bit – I ended up unfollowing the group – way too frustrating – people want things to change, but they don't want to do anything…..uggghhh!

> FB – 4:35 p.m. Facebook:

"Walked into the casino with my headphones on listening to 'All

I do is win'…and lost 50 in 2 minutes. I was in the zone. SMH."

A lot of resentment today.

Wednesday June 14, 2017

10:08 a.m.

"I love you so much. You are amazing."

I had an early client – then did a 15-mile bike ride.

(The night before he called late and asked if I would help him find a counselor. He has been having flashbacks and thinks he needs help processing some past experiences.)

6:43 p.m.

"I know I still have work to do. I am grateful to have the opportunity to learn from my mistakes. I know I can't go to the casino. I told dad that he doesn't need to send me money and that I can take care of myself. Right after that, I got a call for my job!!"

I continue to hear progress and commitment.

Thursday June 15, 2017

I had three clients in the a.m. – two in the evening.

Start a job today!!

Booked a hotel for our New Jersey trip for court.

10:13 p.m. – FB post

"Grateful for where I'm at right now. I'm grateful for the ability to be aware of my mistakes and a chance to make them right. I need to be more mature when dealing with hurt and learn to not try and slander someone because I'm hurt. It was wrong and disrespectful. I'm learning as I grow and growing as I learn. TY people that support me."

Friday June 16, 2017

Worked – only a few clients. It was a good day.

1:43 p.m. – text

"Yesterday I started a new job. Something different than I'm used to or comfortable with. I think I did well and was a little nervous and am looking forward to getting better."

Preparing for our cycling trip for the weekend.

"Today I feel great and am excited for my second day. I feel confident."

Saturday June 17, 2017

Rainy morning – woke up early in anticipation of our ride.

We waited until about 8:30 when the rain stopped.

Rode about 35 miles – Stephen had a lot of pain – we were about 20 miles from our destination.

Sunday June 18, 2017

FATHER'S DAY

Woke up at five at the campsite with Stephen. Had a small breakfast, some Father's Day gifts – and got on the road about 6:30 a.m.

Had a nice rest of the day enjoying shower, resting, out to lunch, and an evening meditation.

Worked a long day – made $130!

Bryan seemed interested in the meditations that we are doing.

Monday June 19, 2017

"Freedom is something that dies, unless it's used." – Hunter S. Thompson

Board meeting.

Evening appointment.

Bryan went to dinner at his sister's house.

Dinner with Heather and Jeff.

Tuesday June 20, 2017

Morning appointments.

New cycling shoes.

Talk with Bryan.

Discussion about Sharon.

Becky.

Doug is struggling.

Emotional – so much has happened.

Bryan realizes that he learned a lot in treatment and is putting it into practice.

Wednesday June 21, 2017

Had two appointments scheduled in the morning, one no-show.

Texted Bryan in the morning.

11:22 a.m.

"Tired of hearing friends struggle from this disease. My close friend is homeless in downtown Boston. I pray he makes it out alive. This is why I keep all my people close to me because any day it can change. At any moment. We talked yesterday. I told him I loved him last night."

11:30 a.m.

"I know…many times I have reflected on what could have been our last words to each other."

Stephen and I talked about trust and how it is impacted by this disease – it truly destroys relationships, trust, judgment of decisions.

Thursday June 22, 2017

Walked in the morning.

First paycheck in two years.

12:32 p.m.

"I get my first paycheck in two years today that I'm picking up myself."

"Oh my God, what a blessing. You must be so proud…I am!!!"

12:37 p.m.

"Yeah, it has. I'm not rushing to get it before work to get high. I'm not even cashing it today.

12:38 p.m.

"So great… changing patterns…good for you!!"

"Yeah, I know. It's awesome."

Had a client appointment and it was a kind of rough one.

Feeling very happy for him – also a little worried – will he be able to handle this?

Facebook post:

"Fuck – just Fuck. I'll be coming to Florida soon."

Facebook messenger – 7:51 p.m.:

"You going to Florida? Is that serious? Hope all is ok."

"I'm ok – don't worry."

"I hope your friends are too…"

"I'll be ok mother, promise."

Friday June 23, 2017

Five appointments through the day -– felt accomplished.

He sent a silly text – a picture of something having twins. He
said it was him and was waiting for me to type something
so he could screen shot my response.

He had said that he wanted to go to the movies – his friend,
roommate, doesn't want to see the movie he wants. I said maybe
we could go to the movies when we go to New Jersey?

"I have an idea – we should go to New York City
– I've never been – just to walk around a little."

Saturday June 24, 2017

We were supposed to do a training ride. Woke up – it was dark
– then it rained – humid. Ended up on the couch; rested all day.

1:16 p.m.

"NYC….woot! ! Can't wait!"

1:22 p.m.

"I know I'm excited now!"

"Yeah, it will be an adventure…"

"That it will."

Sunday June 25, 2017

The night before – he went to the casino – Brendan was with him,
made me feel better, safer.

6:30 a.m. – did a training ride, had a little breakfast.

"Going to work soon. I'll probably talk to you tomorrow."

(I asked him to look into subway stations
from New Jersey to New York for Tuesday.)

Sat by the river for a couple hours, saw some amazing wildlife.

Rode home – it was hot and got sunburned.

Got a call from Bryan – my voicemail was full –

I listened to about 12 saved messages that I still can't erase, and I cried and want Bryan to hear them. These were all messages from times he made it to a detox and telling me he was safe and alive. I remember always feeling relief and love and fear that these might be the last messages.

June 26, 2017

I had five appointments during the day.

> "I think it will be ok. I might just get probation."

I noticed I was distracted – going to court with Bryan tomorrow. I am driving six hours to meet him, then an hour to court – then back to the hotel.

Heather and Jeff came over for dinner – that was nice.

Tuesday June 27, 2017

I woke up several times through the night – looking at the clock.

1:36 a.m. – Woke up from a scary dream – all I remembered was I walked into a room and Bryan was being held against a wall – his arms outstretched, and someone was sticking a needle in his back. He looked at me and said, "It's okay, Mom." I can still see the image.

Started driving at 8:00. Met him at 2:30 at the hotel.

We left for court, got there about four – he bought us snacks.

Met the cop who arrested him. He was nice and seemed happy to see him doing well.

Spent an hour in court. Fines of $700 – no probation, no license loss.

"I'm glad to be done with this; I never have to come back here."

We went to dinner. Definitely too tired to go to New York City.

I drove back – he was too tired – I was exhausted.

Wednesday June 28, 2017

I woke up at 5-6 a.m. and meditated.

Left the room to call Stephen and have a little breakfast.

I was feeling sad and overwhelmed and had a hard time understanding my feelings.

I called – 12:18 p.m.

Are you home?

> "Hi Mom, I just walked in. Thank you for coming with me – you didn't have to do that, and you did. And keep writing the book – it's admiral and a good thing."

I asked him if he wanted me to wait to include him in writing this book – he said he doesn't even remember a lot of stuff.

I left about 9:30 – I was very emotional driving home; not sure why.

Relieved he didn't go to jail.

Grateful to spend a little time with him, sad I won't see him for two months. Realizing there is a lot I don't know about him... what if I don't like him, what if he doesn't like me?

Thursday June 29, 2017

Seven clients during the day.

> Had a CT scan in the a.m. – to check for a concussion.

A little tired, but relieved that I have been able to focus on my work and not be preoccupied with Bryan.

> 2:27 p.m.

> "I opened up a bank account."

I got myself a new counselor – I feel like I need to process some of this past year. I also have resentments still about family members who were not willing to celebrate Bryan's birthday. These are long standing issues for me.

Friday June 30, 2017

Had six clients throughout the day.

One client reported that a family member is now using heroin. Client feels ashamed and confused and a little worried what others will think of her.

I shared a little of personal experience in an effort to offer perspective of the epidemic and who is affected.

12:43 p.m. – text

"Hope you had a good rest and a good morning. I love you."

1:02 p.m.

"I did!! Finally!! Thank goodness, Lol!"

July 2017

Saturday July 1, 2017

Stephen was teaching a Reiki class today.

Work, floods, stress…

I did some work for work and relaxed a little after a busy week.

He called a couple of times stressed about the roads being closed and not being able to deliver pizzas.

Caught up with a friend on the phone; we share a lot of parallels in our lives.

He was highly agitated and then started complaining about his boss; he said he was 'being a jerk.'

"I don't like being disrespected."

I started feeling anxious and worried that these strong emotions would be too much for him to handle and he would act in an impulsive way and quit the job, get fired, or just act out in some way that would lead in a negative direction.

I had to remind myself to not get caught up in that emotion and to trust that 'this is now, not then.' I thought of how I might respond to one of the other children, when I don't worry about their emotions and where they will lead.

6:06 p.m. – text

"6:06…. Hope your afternoon has gone more smoothly…love you!"

"Yeah, it has. I mean all in all. I'm at like $30 in tips. And 7.5 hours, so $100."

"Great! Good job!"

9:19 p.m. – text

"I'm home!"

9:50 p.m.

"Good. Rest well tonight."

9:58 p.m. – text

"I will, mother, I will."

I felt like he built some more strength and maybe confidence in himself and dealing with things. It made it easier for me to not worry. I am grateful to keep having the willingness to let go of my own worries, that aren't helpful to anyone. I feel it will take ongoing practice…just for today.

Sunday July 2, 2017

I walked the dogs, made quiche, did laundry, changed sheets.

He was frustrated with his roommate. He sees some behaviors that are stressing him out and making him nervous. His friend has anxiety, has lots of medications, too many.

Alec got here about noon.

Bryan is upset, and a little worried about the roommate.

We visited and rested, then walked into town.

He worked two long days this week.

We had dinner out on the deck, it was a beautiful evening. Stephen did Tarot card readings for us.

My reading included a male figure close to you: "He is on his path, straight ahead and focused."

He feels good about what he is doing and making his own money.

Thinking more clearly. Seems to be thinking through decisions.

I teared up with gratitude and hope that this is really IT and it will be straight ahead, focused, and positive.

Could it be true?

Do I want to believe it fully?

Monday July 3, 2017

Three-mile walk/run.

Breakfast outside.

Early appointment.

New counselor appointment.

3:11 – text

> He got his debit card – and said, "It's cool, it's awesome."

> 3:14 p.m.

> "I feel grown. I'm doing my laundry, taking care of things on my day off. Took money out of the bank; didn't give it away! Staying grateful for today…last year in jail – now I'm free – but staying in. Learning how to handle situations that before I would make mistakes. Learning how to work things out. Working and taking care of my responsibilities on my days off. Learning/struggling to deal with emotions and situations."

I feel overwhelmed with gratitude. I feel like crying…happy and grateful.

Tuesday July 4, 2017

I went for a bike ride and came back and started to organize a tag sale.

Found some items Bryan might want.

"Set some stuff aside for me and we might use some of it."

I remember it was eight years ago that Bryan had been living with us – went to Boston with friends, got drunk, and ended up in the hospital.

We cooked out and went to the fireworks with Alec and Heather. It was real nice.

Wednesday July 5, 2017

11:08 a.m. – text

"I'm pretty sure I sprained my wrist in my sleep."

Thursday July 6, 2017

3:12 p.m. – "So awesome!!!" (He bought tickets for a Red Sox game at Fenway.)

3:24 p.m.

Doug and Bryan can't wait for this experience. A month ago, I couldn't buy myself anything and was clean but not progressing. Today, I can. Beyond grateful.

6:00 – Facebook:

"I'm killing it today. 3 racks, 100 pizzas done by 6:45"

8:09 p.m.

"What happened to Becky?"

"IDK. She's an ass. Fuck heroin."

11:05 p.m.

"I'm sorry for your pain – I can't sleep knowing you're struggling, so I know there is so little I can do. It hurts and I am tired of all the pain for everyone. I love you so much…"

"I love you too. Don't worry I'll be okay. I'm scared and waiting for her death. It's gonna happen."

"I know it seems like it…I thought the same for you and here you are…it sucks so much not knowing how things will turn out."

"I'm done with it. I'll talk to you tomorrow…I'm out with friends now. . Have to have a good night."

"I am going to try to sleep…I have 6 appts. tomorrow…it's so hard acting like I am fine and can help people, can't help my family or self at times like this…"

"It'll be okay I promise. I'm having fun."

Friday July 7, 2017

5:58 a.m. - texts

"I have white pockets in my throat; can't swallow or talk, my throat is swollen like crazy"

"Oh no….maybe strep? Can you get to the doctors?"

"I'm in so much pain."

"It's so swollen my ear is ringing."

"This is bullshit fuck this!!!!"

"Why??!!?!"

4:03 p.m. – No worries son-shine – It's all good…life happens.

"Overtired and stressed out doesn't help. Is there a walk-in place?"

"I can't even swallow. I can't miss time from work ugh. My Wi-Fi isn't working. I'm literally in so much pain. My ear kills I feel like someone is stabbing my ear."

"I know….if you can get it checked out, if it's strep, they can give you antibiotic, won't have to miss work."

6:33 a.m.

"No, it's so bad."

"Is there someplace that might open at like 8?"

"No, I didn't even sleep."

"I'm over this."

"I know. What does that mean? You're over it?"

"Just being stressed out."

"Yup, it wears ya down. Not to be a broken record, but that's why counseling can help, learn how to manage stress…"

"Yeah, this is what I get."

"Well, it has been a lot lately, it will get better. It's not like you're being punished, people get sick when they get run down, and sometimes just because there are germs and bacteria…"

"I can't even eat. Then this guy is telling me Becky is pregnant. Her friend said she's not pregnant wtf she just had her period."

"I don't know what to say, you can't move forward while staying in some of that chaos."

The conversation ended…he didn't want to talk anymore.

8:02 a.m.

"I called back. When I'm going through this, I don't like talking about this. I'm hurt and angry more than ever. Nothing I have to say about her or the situation will be nice."

"I know I'm sorry. I just don't want to visit you in jail or the cemetery and that's all I see when you are in this state. I know you're hurt, but hurting others will NOT make that any better."

"Yeah, I know."

"I can't do anything to help you and that is hard. I keep praying and I love you and I am here…I'm sad for you all who have been through the horrors of this disease."

"Yeah, and who been hurt like this."

"I'm battling not going to get codeine for my throat, I am. I know I can get pmoth and codeine and be messed up. I know."

"You are loved and adored by many…accept that instead of chasing her, who's not willing to give you the love you deserve and appreciate you."

"Yeah, I'm not chasing her anymore; she's dead to me."

"Go to the doctor…you can live with some hurt feelings and work through them…they won't kill you, the drugs will, even if it starts with some cough medicine. I will check in with you later…stay strong and focused. You have so many plans and opportunities."

"Okay, I won't. Love you."

3:00

Setting up online banking

4:00

"Sorry about this morning, I love you. That won't happen again."

"I'm rooting for you and praying."

4:48

"Yeah, I know, I need to handle this better."

Saturday July 8, 2017

Stephen and I went to a Holistic Fair.

I was working on the book – feelings all stirred up, irritated.

10:05 a.m.

Call – "Good morning – I'm ready for work. I made $80 yesterday."

12:45 p.m. – text

Ignore my post. ("I'm coming back to Florida.")

12:46 p.m.

I'm not on Facebook.

"Ok, don't want to worry you."

"Remember my friend Alan from HS? He said maybe
I could coach with him."

"Let's go to MA and we can work on the book, and you can meet
with Alan."

Sunday July 9, 2017

Alec left.

Stephen and I went for a bike ride – 20 miles.

Then we went to the grocery store, I sat out at the tag sale – wrote
notes for work.

Called Bryan to check in and begin to make a plan to connect in
Massachusetts to discuss the book.

"Yeah – sounds good. We can meet on my days off."

9:23 p.m. – Facebook message:

"Hey, going to sleep, hope you had a good day at work. Rest
well...call when you wake up. Love you so much."

9:58 p.m.

"I did. I was so tired. I feel much better after a nap.
I love you. Good night."

Monday July 10, 2017

1:48 p.m. – text

"In case you didn't know. I love you, and I'm so grateful for
you."

2:00 p.m.

"Ooh, thank you...I do know and same back at you my son-shine."

"Thank you. I'm napping/relaxing. I'll call you after."

9:33 p.m. – Facebook message:

"Did you get a chance to check with Alan about the 24-25? Rest well. I have appointments between 8-12 tomorrow. Love you!"

9:35 p.m.

"Not yet. Call me when you're out. I caught up on rest/sleep this afternoon. Thank God. I love you."

Tuesday July 11, 2017

1:30 p.m.

"I'm around – just checking in. Hope you are well. Love you!"

1:33 p.m.

"at doctor – call in a few."

He sent a photo of the kitchen and the dirty dishes his roommate doesn't clean. "I feel for you, I do know, it's hard living with someone – takes time to work it out..."

2:30 p.m.

"I'm sorry – I'm a little annoyed. I gotta go clean the dishes at home and sink cuz, it's disgusting. None of it's mine."

7:46 p.m.

"I'm getting ready to share an initial sample of the book with some people..."

7:48 p.m.

"Yeah. I'll read it. Just let me know. Has anyone else donated?"

"No, and I haven't put anything out in a while."

"Yeah, I can't handle it yet. Get me on one of these shows, I'll expose every one of them and tell the truth."

It's a bit frustrating but we'll plug away.

"I'll put up money soon."

"That's very awesome of you, ty…<3 get yourself stable first."

"We will figure it out. I love you. Have a good night."

"Yes, we will…love you too!"

Wednesday July 12, 2017

12:24 p.m.

"Did you email that to me?"

"No, not yet, I had a meeting."

"Alright, please do."

Sent – the intro, April letters and the first draft of August 2016.

1:49 p.m.

"Got it"

2:19 p.m.

"I'm reading it now."

3:01 p.m.

"When you get to February it's gonna be tough. I have some ideas."

3:54 p.m.

"Hotel is booked! Woot!"

6:47 p.m.

$50 donation – from Stephen's mom.

6:50 p.m.

Awesome!

Thursday July 13, 2017

12:39 p.m.

"Will you help me move into my own place? I can't stay in Oneida."

3:38 p.m. – text

"You're so strong, you deserve all good things. You are doing a good job; I am proud of your efforts and changes. As always, I will help in any way I can to move forward in your life, whatever that is."

3:40 p.m.

"I know you will, thank you. I won't stop fighting for my life. I can't I love you and thank you. I'm sorry."

10:29 p.m. – phone call

11:05 p.m. – I saw a missed call, called back.

"Me and Brendan had a fight – I had to leave."

(Then there was an incident at a gas station, and the police were called.)

Friday July 14, 2017

I had an appointment, no-show.

11:56 a.m. – text

"One more incident with Brendan and I'm gone. I'm gonna talk to Sarah and see if she'll help for a few days."

Went for a bike ride.

12:13 p.m.

"I have some thinking to do."

Sent an intro sample of the book to a friend and got some nice feedback.

Three appointments in the afternoon.

Bryan went to work early – sounds focused and determined.

After a conversation later in the day it was clear he is thinking about options, thinking about where he has been and where he wants to go – using perspective.

I continue to be reminded that this is now – not then. He is growing every day. Using his supports – thinking about others.

Saturday July 15, 2017

Sat out at the tag sale for a bit.

I did some reading.

NOTHING DOCUMENTED

Went to dinner for our anniversary.

Sunday July 16, 2017

I went up to New Portland and mowed the lawn.

Stephen worked on the Wellness Center.

We relaxed most of the afternoon.

11:21 a.m.

"11:11 <3"

5:50 p.m.

"I continue to be grateful for you and proud of your every day. Never forget."

5:52 p.m.

"I know mother, I was just thinking along those lines. I love you."

"Thank God it's my Friday."

Went for a swim in the evening.

Monday July 17, 2017

Five appointments through the day.

Took care of errands – depositing money, paid fine to New Jersey.

We had a practitioner come to look at our space for the Tarot and Tea event!

Heather came over and we had dinner – hung out on the deck – it was nice and relaxing.

He got a tattoo – prayer hands, with 2-3 – date of his flat line.

I had a dream – early in the a.m. Bryan said he was going to his friend's program for two weeks – I was really upset. Was it prophecy? Just a dream?

Tuesday July 18, 2017

8:00 a.m. appointment.

Board meeting.

Anniversary…12 years!

Stephen didn't go to work because of rain.

We ate lunch. Rested. Relaxed.

1:30 p.m.

Doctor appointment.

"Visited family. Grandma was happy to see me. Went to see other family too."

"Hanging out with the kids – they were fun, happy to see me."

He got "the call" about Becky.

4:17 p.m.

He called; Becky's on life support. Sobbing...

My heart sank...what will this mean for him? Will he be able to handle the sadness and powerlessness?

Stephen had a 4:30 estimate – I had an appointment.

We had dinner...Bryan called.

7:00 p.m.

"I know I did everything I could."

Those are healthy words...how will he handle it if she dies?

Will he be ok?

"I feel so sad, angry, miserable – no one will answer my calls!!"

Will he want to go to Florida?

Wednesday July 19, 2017

I had three appointments during the day.

Bryan called at 7:38 a.m.

"There's a fire in the apartment. I don't know what happened; there was just smoke. I think he fell asleep with a cigarette. I wanted to call 911 and Brendan got mad. I didn't care – grabbed the kitten and called anyway. Then fell back to sleep."

"When it rains, it pours...hang in there..."

11:26 text

"I'm confused"

Thursday July 20, 2017

Stephen did some shopping.

> Two-year anniversary of dating Becky.

> Becky came out of a coma.

> Feeling happy, relieved, nervous – "I don't want to go through it again."

No appointments until late afternoon.

Thank God – I feel stressed and trying to stay positive, strong, and supportive, and trusting of Bryan.

> I ordered a plane ticket for him to go to Florida – he is excited to see cats, dad, and Becky.

He said he's not going to cut our visit short.

> 7:51 p.m.

> "I can't do this anymore. I don't want to feel this way."

"You gonna pick up?"

> "I'm seriously considering it."

I can't keep doing this…he has a choice of two roads. I guess we both have choices to make.

Friday July 21, 2017

> "I wish I could have been there – I am upset."

> 1:56 p.m. – text

> "Fine is paid."

Saturday July 22, 2017

> Woke up late – in a rush to get to work.

> Talked to Becky on the way – video-chatted.

"I felt happy – I knew her brain was ok, and she was better because she flipped me off."

Made me laugh.

I was angry.

"Didn't get to talk to Brendan about the living situation – I am not sure this is the best situation for both of us."

"Good day at work though – got some positive feedback from co-worker."

Sunday July 23, 2017

"Work sucked – I didn't want to be there."

"Lost out on an $8 tip – frustrated."

"I talked to people about the things that upset me."

Video chatted with a friend from Florida.

Post on Facebook:

"I don't like being judged."

"Felt good to talk with my friend. I feel more c omfortable with myself and who I am."

Monday July 24, 2017

Woke up early; left at 5:30 for Massachusetts – had breakfast with my sister for her birthday.

It's a difficult relationship for me.

Went to the doctor – got a prescription for Hep C medication.

Then got gas and headed to MA. For quick trip. Challenges with roommate.

Checked into the hotel.

Bad weather and bad traffic.

I did some scheduling for work.

Rested a bit.

Met Beth and Alec for dinner.

Bryan arrived about 2:30 – so happy to see him!

Went to dinner with Alec and Beth.

He visited with some of his friends.

A little sad to not see Bryan more – but happy he is getting to spend time with his friends.

Went to bed at 9:15.

"Happy to be with my family and friends."

Tuesday July 25, 2017

Stephen and I went to the reservoir, picked up some Dunkin Donuts.

Came back to the room – we all showered and packed our stuff.

It was nice to just chat and hang out. We are all going back to our lives – I still have pangs – when will I see him again?

Words for book:

"Enjoyed having food and spending time with family."

Going to Six Flags with a friend.

Ended up going to an arcade with his friend.

We went to lunch together – Stephen did a Tarot reading – it was positive about action and changes.

He left West Springfield at 7 – got home about 11 p.m.

Wednesday July 26, 2017

I had four appointments during the day.

Becky was supposed to go to Bill's before flying back to California – she did not and took off.

11:22 a.m.

"It's time to move on, Mom. I won't go through it again.
I have a choice now. I'm choosing this. I'm not mad."

12:31 p.m.

"She hurt dad – he's so upset. I feel protective of him.
Just like when I was a kid."

12:33 p.m.

"Maybe you need to let him grow up and both be adults and be responsible for your own actions and feelings."

Thursday July 27, 2017

NOTHING RECORDED

NOTHING RECORDED

Friday July 28, 2017

I had six appointments through the day.

2:03 p.m.

"I'm having anxiety attack."

3:00 p.m.

Went to the doctor; said he cried to the nurse and felt better.

I had a missed call from him at 5:29 a.m.

4:00 p.m.

He was at a friend's house and said it wasn't the best option but better than sleeping in the car.

"I can't go back to that job."

8:37 p.m.

Are you there?

Settled in?

11:03 p.m.

"Yeah, sorry, sheesh, sorry."

Saturday July 29, 2017

Terrible night's sleep.

Missed call from Bill at 10:07 p.m.

Saw the text from Bryan.

"I don't know what to do. I don't know where I should go. I'm thinking about going back to Florida."

We got up, ate breakfast. I felt sullen.

Went for a bike ride – cried twice while out there.

"Mom, I know you're afraid, but I am not going back there to use or do the same stuff. I just feel like it will be better with more options for me. When I make enough money, I will pay for your plane ticket. I don't want to go through what I did in the past and I don't want to put you through that either. I had a ½ a Xanax last night and I want you to know it's not any more than that. I will stay in touch with you the whole time."

Feeling sad – so unsure of what's ahead.

Rested in the afternoon.

Felt a little better by the end of the day.

He made his decision – he sounds different still – this is now not then. I want to be encouraging and supportive.

Sunday July 30, 2017

He left and returned to Florida.

Monday July 31, 2017

NOTHING RECORDED....I'M SO TIRED

END OF THIS PART OF OUR STORY

To The Addict: I Am Your Mom

Karen Hardy

I hate diseases. I hate the obsession and compulsion of addiction. I hate the way it kills families and individuals. I wish recovery and peace for all affected.

Allow me to introduce myself: I am your Mom. I carried you in my belly for nine months and brought you into this world. My life revolved around your every breath from that moment on. I came to know everything about you: your smell, your sounds, your movements. I fed, bathed, housed, and clothed you and cared for your needs when you couldn't do it yourself.

I was there when you were awake and when you were asleep. I was there to encourage you and teach you about the world. I wiped your nose and your tears and tickled your belly while we laughed together.

You are my history and I yours. Your future is ahead of you and I will be there to travel every step with you, high or low. In your heart is love, which your disease has stolen slowly and with a promise of 'better things.' Your disease lies.

Your disease wants you to believe I am the enemy. It assures you that it is there for you always. It hates all the good things that I want for you and know you can have.

Even though your disease is always there, so am I. Look around at our world and you will see how strong Moms are…they are a force not to be reckoned with. I will fight with you and for you against this disease that threatens so much. With love and support we will win.

Final Thoughts from Karen

As the year that this book covered ended, the roller coaster did not. Bryan returned to Florida; his addiction continued and seemed to worsen. He had done well but there was a lot of pressure in his living situation, and as I later found out, he had been using some. He had gained some independence and confidence but had not made significant inner changes toward recovery.

In August 2017, things were increasingly spiraling out of control. One night after hearing from his father that the ambulance had been called because he was overdosing (his father was not home), I talked to Bryan. He sounded frantic and was insistent that he wasn't overdosing. He did not want the police or ambulance to come get him. I was so afraid and felt so helpless. I asked him, "If I came down there will you come back to Maine with me, and we will drive your car up from Florida?" He said yes. I booked a plane ticket for the following day, and we did just that. I remember not wanting to tell many people what I was doing, especially people in the recovery community. Many people think it's a mistake to bring your adult child with an addiction into your home. I understand, a lot of bad things can and do happen, but I was determined to do everything I could do to help my son. I drove most of the way; he was high or sick a lot of the way. It was the longest, and scariest drive I have ever taken and feels like a blur when I think about it now.

The first month he was here in Maine was a bit rocky, and he almost left more than once, but he didn't. During those first months, he got high more than once. One night , he was supposed to be home, and I woke up to him not home. I called him and he said he was leaving because he got high. I said, "Bryan just come home, we will figure this out." That was not the response he expected and in that moment I felt compassion for him and belief in those words that clearly landed for him the way they were intended....with love.

Today, (December 2022) he has been heroin free for five years. He continues to work on his recovery daily, as do I. The changes he has made are truly astounding, and we talk regularly about how he became addicted and how he has made the changes. One thing I have learned is that there are actions that can be taken that are helpful to the addicted person, some that may be less helpful, and the rhyme or reason to who changes and when is a bit mysterious. I said to Bryan many times that I am in this fight with him, and we will fight together. The fight for life and recovery with addiction has two sides, and it is important for family members to keep the focus on their side of the fight. Self-care, increasing knowledge, having an understanding, and an encouraging support network are all things that I believe are crucial to creating a better environment for recovery to take place. My journey of recovery has included all those things. Most recently, around the time Bryan was coming to Maine, I began to learn about the Internal Family Systems model that I credit to making shifts within myself that created the space for us to both heal from our respective and combined traumatic experiences.

In August of 2021 I delivered a TEDx talk about Bryan's and my experience with his addiction. He and I talk about how we can continue to recover and share our story. I pray for all those who continue to struggle and that all can find peace and healing from whatever pain they carry. I encourage people to continue to explore inside and outside themselves to find what best works for them. Don't stop. Do what you can live with. We all have qualities of compassion, courage, and confidence inside of us that can be so helpful in this process; access those, figure out what might be blocking them, and there's nothing you can't do.

Final Thoughts from Bryan

When I initially wrote this part, I had only 8.5 months without using heroin/opiates (my drug of choice or DOC) and my goal was to be able to live what I perceive to be a normal life. I now have about 5.25 years without using. I chose a different route (therapy first and Suboxone so I didn't die in the process) than the commonly (AA/NA). I struggled with AA/NA for numerous reasons, but the main reason being that it takes me too long to trust random people to go through the steps with and I kept failing that way and I did not want to die. Through help from my family, I have been able to achieve most of the goals I had set for myself. I came to Maine and bought into my recovery. I will share a little about myself and my journey from living a life where I thought I might die each day, to where I am at now: happy and grateful for the people and animals in my life.

This book is extremely important to both my mom and I, but it's more important to the person reading this. I can look back on it at any point and keep some memories fresh in my mind that I think are important because it keeps me grounded, no matter how bad things get when I'm not using, I can look back and realize that it is so much better than it was. In the time this book was written, I overdosed three times, along with having gone into a drug induced psychosis causing blackouts, I witnessed upwards of 15 overdoses, and I revived each person, and I was told I died by the EMT after one overdose on 2/3/2017 after overdosing the day before in the same county and ending up at the same hospital. I don't say this to share "War Stories" but to show the depths of MY addiction as each persons' rock bottom is different just like each persons' recovery should look different because we are all different people.

I will go through a condensed version of how I was able to get to where I am today, at least in my recovery from opiates and other mental health issues I found out about along the way.

It was August 18th, 2017, and I was in Port St. Lucie, Florida, staying with my dad. I had sent a message out saying I didn't want to live anymore by sending someone an image of four needles loaded with heroin. I was ready to die. He had called me, freaking out and screaming that he is calling the cops/ambulance and was coming home from where he was. All hell then broke loose.

I went into a blackout, and I destroyed the house by breaking my bed frame, the doors on my closet, and tried to break anything in my way. I even head butted a door open. I then ran across the street to the little shopping plaza and threw out my drugs and then went back to my dad's.

The cops and ambulance showed up and tried to either arrest me or keep me hospitalized, but they could not because I had no drugs or paraphernalia on my person. I was told I was either going away to jail or the hospital, it was my choice. While I was at the hospital, the doctors got on the phone with my mom after my dad showed up and called her because he didn't know what to do. The doctors told me that I was given the option to either stay hospitalized because I was a threat to myself or others OR agree to go with my mom the next day and drive to Maine. My mom bought a plane ticket right then and there for the next day and just like that, I was driving to Maine the next day and had no idea what my future held but all I could think about was, "Fuck! I'm about to be sick tomorrow and must figure something out to change that."

The next day was August 19th, 2017, and my mom landed in Florida around nine that morning to drive right back to Maine with me, her heroin-addicted son who is on the cusp of death. I am supposed to meet her at the airport which I did do, but not before making a few stops before meeting her. On the way, I picked up what I thought was enough heroin to last until I made it to Maine, but boy was I wrong. I ran out before I even left the state of Florida…

I can't imagine what that drive was like for my mom. I stopped every hour to "use the bathroom." Then, I grew more and more sick from there on out with only 10 mg of Suboxone, which is a synthetic opiate that stops withdrawal and lets you function without being high (which you can't take for at least 12 hours after the last time using, or it could put you in something known as precipitated withdrawal which can be worse than regular withdrawal). So, I was in full blown withdrawal for the next eight hours or so until we got to Camden, New Jersey, where we stayed for the night and ordered a pizza (which is my favorite food, and I could hardly eat a slice from feeling sick). I decided to try to take a 2 mg Suboxone and hope it would help a little. It did, and I slept as best as I could until we left around 3:30 a.m. when we packed up and left Camden to go to Connecticut to get my mom's car and finish the drive to Maine.

We made it to Maine finally on Sunday afternoon. The Suboxone was barely helping, and all I could think about was finding a way to get more money to get high, so I wouldn't be sick, and I thought I could control my habit and ween myself off heroin by doing a little less each time (brilliant idea!). I found some money and I was heading out for my seven hours round trip to Fitchburg, Massachusetts, just to get a little bit of heroin to not be sick but did it all that night and was going to be sick.

My first week living in Maine, I set a goal to get a job so I could save enough money to move to California on my own and get together with an ex (which looking back was an awful idea, but it motivated me at the time), and I found a job. I got hired at Subway, making it the tenth different Subway I have worked at, in a total of four different states.

Then, one night I drove out to Lawrence, Massachusetts, to get high after my first 80-dollar check came in. I left the house at 3pm and I got home around 10 or 11 p.m. I was doing a shot and I hit an artery in my arm, and it was one of (if not the) worst pain I have ever felt in my life. It felt as if someone was using a blow torch on my right forearm and burning it from the inside out. The ambulance seemingly took hours to get to the house as I was screaming at the top of my lungs in pain. This night in the hospital was important at the time and started shifting things for me.

The following day, I had work at 9 a.m. and was in the hospital until roughly 5 a.m. I remember getting a few hours of sleep before work and was able to work my full shift. After work, I received a phone call right when I got out of work that day (from the hospital I was at the night before). They gave me information for all different types of places, from needle exchanges to medically assisted treatment programs, to outpatient programs and AA or NA meetings and more. Up to that point, I had failed doing the AA and NA way many times over and knew it wasn't right for me.

So, I decided to take the medically assisted treatment (MAT) route. I went right to the place that holds groups and prescribes Suboxone and set up an appointment that day to see their doctor the following Tuesday. I only had to make it through five days of withdrawal to get there. I made it through, but they said, "You must wait two more days to see the doctor because this week she is not in until Thursday, we are sorry." My heart sank and I felt sick again. I had not slept for a few days, I struggle to eat as it is, but nothing was appetizing, I weighed about 135 pounds, I was in pain, I was sweating and freezing at the same time, and I didn't like feeling my feelings at this point in time. I did what every drug addict does... I drove 3.5 hours to Massachusetts to get high. I kept driving to Massachusetts because I knew I wanted to get clean in Maine and didn't want to find someone to get drugs from here as I thought it might help not having somewhere locally to get drugs from.

That last day using heroin, I easily could have died. After leaving Massachusetts, I ended up getting lost driving home, even falling asleep while driving causing me to swerve off the road only to wake up from the bumps in the breakdown lane. I took a couple wrong turns and ended up in New Hampshire, and after getting back on track, I ended up in Lewiston at the Ramada Inn around 5 a.m. I called my mom and former stepdad to come and pick me up because I couldn't see straight and was going to crash. I went into the bathroom with every intention to do a shot of heroin, and I got it ready but fell out on the toilet before I could do a shot (thank God too because I couldn't handle any more at that time and likely would have died). I was in there for at least 40 minutes before my mom called when she arrived at or around 6:00 a.m. I came out of a deep sleep to the sound of my cell phone ringing, in a panic and still on the toilet with my drugs and drug paraphernalia clutched in my hands. I ran out to see her happy as hell thinking (for some reason) that she would be happy to see me too. She was not (obviously). I was a complete wreck, and I had to be to work at 10:00 a.m. that morning. I was sent home at 10:30 because I didn't look well, I looked sick... But I wasn't sick, I was high. I proceeded to use all day, falling out left and right and miraculously did not overdose. This was September 13th, 2017, and the last day I used heroin.

September 14th, 2017. This is my clean date. When I used this time around, my mom didn't kick me out, didn't threaten to kick me out, didn't try to ship me off to my hundredth treatment program; she just wanted to keep me alive by any means. She was willing to do anything and worked diligently to make sure she was in the best position to give me the unconditional love a child needs from their parent. What I learned from her is that unconditional love is the best remedy.

My Recovery

My recovery in the beginning did not look at all what it looks like now. At first, I went to a place that held groups twice a week and I saw an individual group leader that would do check-in's weekly. They prescribed Suboxone weekly. I did not have insurance, so I had to pay out of pocket (with help from my mom) and had to wait until I could apply for insurance during their open window of enrollment for Maine insurance. I initially thought I would just be on Suboxone for a year and was extremely insecure about doing my recovery this way because in all the 50 or more treatment facilities I have been at, they put down Suboxone as a crutch. The sad truth is, there is stigma within the recovery community surrounding medically assisted treatment (aka MAT), but I bet every one of my friend's families would prefer their children alive and on Suboxone than dead. That's the way I viewed it, and I wanted to live and have a family, along with the other people who matter back in my life.

When I went to group therapy, I was nice and friendly to everyone, but I didn't make friends with them because that has always led to something bad happening. I participated in my group, got my Suboxone weekly, and I worked as many hours as possible at Subway. I used work as a tool when I was triggered or bored and felt like using. If I couldn't go to work, I got back into sports and playing sports video games, all things I enjoyed doing before I was getting high. I knew this wasn't enough though and I needed to do more because the groups were just surface level stuff and I had a lot of baggage (truthfully, my mom kept pushing me and after two months I gave in to getting a therapist).

I started seeing a therapist and found a doctor who prescribes Suboxone and is my PCP, all in one place! I knew what my goals were and that I wanted to get to a place where I could feel like a normal human being who is allowed to have a margarita when I go out to eat or have a drink watching the NY Giants or Yankees play. I knew I wasn't an alcoholic in the sense that if I drink one drink at home, I won't be tempted to drink the whole case of beer or start hiding beers in my room, BUT, if I am not careful, I have the tendencies to take anything to the extreme (I also didn't drink for the first four or five months and hate the feeling of being drunk and will throw up after three drinks). Everyone is different, and I have seen people not able to drink without burning everything down around them, so if that is you DON'T do that, please.

When I met my first therapist in Maine, I told her I was not willing to do relapse prevention because relapse was not an option, and I knew I needed to get to the shit that led me to using drugs in the first place. I was motivated like never before and determined to get better and find a way that worked for me and be a "normal" person. I knew what I wanted and where I was going and fully believed in the laws of attraction, and what you put out in this world is what you get back. I set goals for myself to get a job, work my way up at the job, move out when I got my taxes, pay off my court fees from my New Jersey arrest, and get a cat when I move out. I knocked one goal out after another, and along the way I met my now wife, Melanie. I also decided to go to school for Mental Health at Kennebec Valley Community College and Melanie had sat down with me to help me with the application process.

Thankfully, Melanie had not had a bad experience with someone who used drugs and was naïve to how little time three months is, but I acted like I had three years. I was very confident that I was moving forward without the drugs, and she believed in me and saw something in me back then (Thank God). She had just graduated college and was looking for a teaching position for kindergarten through 5th graders. We moved in together after three months of dating into an awfully small apartment in a rough area with wild and crazy neighbors. It was a struggle for a while. One of my friends moved to Maine, and his mom bought a duplex for us which was a huge upgrade for us at the time, but it lasted all of eight months because the situation was not right for us and didn't feel safe for me so we abruptly moved into a small bedroom in my mom's house. That didn't go as planned either and I thought my relationship was the issue and broke up with Melanie for three weeks and she found a small quaint trailer, about 40 minutes north of where I was. I ended up moving into the small trailer with Mel, and the pandemic happened, which only made our relationship stronger.

When I got back together with Melanie, I had an epiphany. I realized all the issues I thought Melanie and I were having were instead my issues I was projecting onto Melanie. This is when I realized the depths of the issues I had been dealing with, and I started to find some answers that made sense to me. During this time, I was taking the Trauma class at school, and I realized the trauma I had been dealing with this whole time, without knowing. During class one day, I couldn't hold back my tears and had to run out of class because I couldn't stop crying. My mom had been telling me that I should get a trauma therapist, and I thought she was exaggerating. This is the point where real change started to occur as I realized therapy wasn't about that one hour you spend at the office talking to your therapist; it is about the other 167 hours and what you do when triggered during those times. At this time, things started clicking for me in my own therapy and under-standing, but I was still struggling with my relationships with my mom and dad, but Melanie and I had a much better relationship since this epiphany.

Around this time, I started seeing a therapist that has helped me in ways other therapists had not done before. She noticed that I had a whole bunch of different diagnoses (ADD, anxiety, depression, substance use disorder, and PTSD) and was looking into whether there was a personality disorder as well. When she read the nine things to look for to get a diagnosis of Borderline Personality Disorder, I finally felt like I had a diagnosis that explained a lot and that I felt was accurate (I was diagnosed with ADD at 12 and I never thought it was right). This diagnosis along with Intermittent Explosive Disorder, have helped make me feel less shameful for my reactions because I understand where they derive from (trauma).

I say all of that to say this: I knew I had to get to the root of what led me to wanting a substance to make me feel comfortable in my own skin. As I have gotten older and matured, I have gotten increasingly more comfortable with myself, but it also took a lot of work and effort to get to this point. I currently see three therapists, go to my doctor's office once a month, and going to gastroenterology for my stomach. My body fought off Hep C on its own (I was going to get the meds to cure it when I tested negative for it), and I have a psychiatrist who I see monthly as well. I am working toward coming off Suboxone and starting a family with my wife to add to our dog and four cats (plus one in heaven, RIP Vader).

I will be writing my own book next, so I don't want to over share here but kept it very condensed. I hope whoever is reading this that is struggling or has a loved on struggling please shows them love and empathy and try to understand that they may be in some real pain that you are not aware of.

Words of Encouragement from Bryan Massey

Most people in recovery failed at it their first time and likely the second and third time as well. I don't say this to encourage relapse but to let you know that if you are still alive, you still have a chance to be successful. I didn't go the traditional route of AA because it did not work for me, and I am thankful I found a doctor that I am grateful every day for along with my mom and wife who supported me the past five years and helped me get to this point. Find yourself a support network that will fight with you instead of making you the scapegoat or making your life harder and put your recovery before everything else. Everything you put before your recovery will be the first things you lose if you relapse. I hated this cliché (and others) from AA but a lot of them are clichés because there is truth and wisdom in them. I had a wedding ceremony in Las Vegas, and I had an online therapy appointment on the morning of my wedding ceremony. This cliché was in my mind, and I firmly believe that without putting my therapy and mental health first, I wouldn't be afforded the opportunity to have a wedding ceremony or the countless other blessings I have had these past five plus years.

About the Author

Karen Hardy is a mental health and addiction counselor with a private practice in Belgrade, Maine. Born in New Haven, Connecticut, she worked as a correctional counselor in the Connecticut state prison system for 20 years. She earned an addictions certification while working in prison, and then earned a master's degree in counseling psychology upon retirement. She has a strong interest in helping the families and loved ones of with people with addiction. She and her husband have four children and a dog. In 2019, Karen and Stephen did some section hiking on the Appalachian Trail for overdose awareness. Karen continues to use her experiences in her life to bring awareness, support, and healing to others who struggle.